Adolescent Group Therapy

Adolescent Group Therapy

A SOCIAL COMPETENCY MODEL

George R. Holmes,
Robert V. Heckel,
and
Lucille Gordon

PRAEGER

New York
Westport, Connecticut
London

Library of Congress Cataloging-in-Publication Data

Holmes, George R.
Adolescent group therapy : a social competency model / George R. Holmes, Robert V. Heckel, and Lucille Gordon.
p. cm.
Includes bibliographical references.
Includes index.
ISBN 0-275-94024-1 (alk. paper)
1. Group psychotherapy for teenagers. I. Heckel, Robert V. II. Gordon, Lucille. III. Title.
[DNLM: 1. Psychotherapy, Group—in adolescence. WM 463 H751a]
RJ505.G7H65 1991
616.89'152'0835—dc20
DNLM/DLC
for Library of Congress 91-2693

British Library Cataloguing in Publication Data is available.

Library of Congress Catalog Card Number: 91-2693
ISBN: 0-275-94024-1

First published in 1991

Praeger Publishers, One Madison Avenue, New York, NY 10010
An imprint of Greenwood Publishing Group, Inc.

Printed in the United States of America

The paper used in this book complies with the Permanent Paper Standard issued by the National Information Standards Organization (Z39.48-1984).

10 9 8 7 6 5 4 3 2 1

To Elizabeth Anne, William Francis, Elaine,
Georgia Lynne, and Mark Timothy

CONTENTS

PREFACE

Over the past twenty-five years, George R. Holmes has worked with Robert V. Heckel, as student, as colleague, and as co-author of articles on individual and group psychotherapy. Our productive and scholarly relationship has been enhanced by our close personal friendship over the years. Now we turn our efforts to a book on adolescent group therapy.

A major inspiration for this book has been Holmes's clinical work as the co-director of the inpatient adolescent group therapy program at the William S. Hall Psychiatric Institute in Columbia, South Carolina. Therapy responsibilities were shared with Lucy Gordon, A.C.S.W. Our work generated many of the clinical techniques in treatment and innovations in training discussed in this book.

Heckel's expertise as a teacher and clinical pracititioner in group dynamics and group psychotherapy contributes to the literature review and research components of this book. His work as a consultant to adolescent group psychotherapy programs in the South Carolina Department of Mental Health and at the South Carolina Department of Youth Services adds significantly to the clinical perspective of the book.

In addition to the clinical experiences that have shaped our emerging model of adolescent group therapy, numerous other factors have played an important role. From a historical basis, we have each been influenced by individuals and events. It is impossible to credit each person and event, and for this reality we apologize.

For Holmes, former professors and good friends Elmore Martin, Racine Brown, William Rothstein, and Myles Friedman have given valuable consultation and support through the development of this book. A significant experience in a basic human interaction group at the National Training Laboratory in Bethel, Maine, expanded Holmes's interest in using group therapy as a technique to promote psychological health among adolescent psychiatric inpatients. Finally, for both Holmes and Gordon, the 1978 Primary Prevention Conference on Social Competency held at the University of Vermont confirmed the theoretical and practical position that social competency development is a central ingredient in adolescent group work.

Heckel's experience in basic human interaction at the National Training Laboratory played a major role in expanding his already established interest in group psychotherapy. His early work in clinical practice, which focused on children, adolescents, and parents' struggles, set the stage for his strong interest in the adolescent developmental years and for his later clinical work with groups of teenagers.

Gordon's clinical and teaching experience in systems-oriented family therapy significantly shaped her view of adolescent "psychopathology" and helped with the evolution of our group therapy approach. The theoretical perspectives of family therapists such as Haley, Hoffman, and Papp encouraged Gordon and Holmes to explore and define problem behaviors in terms of the adaptive or protective functions they served in the adolescents' family and social systems.

The data for this book come from the research literature on group dynamics, group psychotherapy with adolescents, the psychological and psychiatric literature on adolescent development, and more than one hundred adolescents seen in group therapy. The adolescent patients have been our teachers, and we have a strong feeling of kinship with those young people and a sense of gratitude for what they have given us during their time in group therapy. Consequently, we feel there is a mandate operating for us to capture both the research literature and clinical data in a useful way for current and future practitioners of adolescent group psychotherapy.

Appreciation is expressed to the Unversity of South Carolina School of Medicine for Holmes's sabbatical in 1986, which enabled him to start the process of writing this book. Thanks go to Josephine Evans, who typed the initial version of the manuscript. Special appreciation and thanks are tendered to Melissa Mills Herring for her skilled editing and typing of the final version of the manuscript.

Adolescent Group Therapy

1

INTRODUCTION

Our youth began with tears and sighs,
With seeking what we could not find;
We sought and knew not what we sought;
We marvel, now we look behind.

—Andrew Lang
Ballade of Middle Age

PRIMARY PURPOSE

The primary purpose of our book is to present an approach to adolescent group therapy in which the group process, and the specific tactics and strategies used, are geared to faciliating the development of interpersonal social competency in each member.

The literature on primary prevention of the 1960s and 1970s (White, 1976) and the developmental psychology research on the normal family (Baumrind, 1978) emphasize the centrality of social competency development for all adolescents, whether they are psychiatric inpatients or outpatients or are not even in formal treatment.

Social competency development for these researchers acts as a preventive force against the development of particular conduct disorders or other types of mental illness. In White's original monograph, the term *competence* had the broad definition of "an organism's capacity to interact effectively with its environment," whereas the term *feelings of efficacy* refers to "the satisfaction that comes from producing the effects."

Again, the concepts of effectance development and social competency building gained popular acceptance in the primary prevention area as techniques for the prevention of mental illness, and the concepts certainly have particular applicability to the developing adolescent.

A sampling of the research literature over the past three decades reveals that research on social competency continues to be the focus of interest for a broad range of researchers. Social competency development has been investigated by developmental psychologists with populations of preschoolers, grade school youngsters, adolescents, and college students.

Clinical psychologists, educators, and social workers have studied social competency development or social competency deficits in special populations such as depressed psychiatric patients or mentally handicapped persons. A wide variety of methods was used to assess social competency in the studies reviewed, including psychometric scales, peer nomination, sociometric choice, group status, expert ratings, and social problem-solving skills.

Even though social competency development continues to be an active area of research, there is still no single operational definition of social competency agreed upon by a majority of researchers.

In her paper, Baumrind (1978) offers a definition of social competency that has relevance to both developmental psychologists and clinicians treating teenagers. She indicates that the adolescent must (1) begin to delay gratification without going to the extreme of absolutely denying sexual pleasure; (2) start the process of taking the other person's perspective without a denial of one's own view of the world; and (3) be open to obeying reasonable laws while confronting injustices and unreasonableness in various control measures.

For Baumrind, this social competency development unfolds in the context of each adolescent's family as the teenagers interact, with their parents particularly. Citing her earlier work (Baumrind, 1966, 1968), she concludes that of the three types of parental approaches—authoritarian, permissive, and authoritative—authoritative control, which focuses on directing the adolescent's activities in a rationally oriented manner, allows the greatest amount of social competency to develop.

The parent or educator using authoritative control, according to Baumrind, interacts in the following ways with teenagers: (1) encourages verbal give-and-take and shares the rationale behind certain policies, and gets input from the adolescent when conformity to a policy is refused; (2) recognizes that the combination of autonomous self-will and disciplined conformity is of central value in any transation with an adolescent; (3) is authoritatively able to enforce the adult perspective but recognizes the teenager's interests and special ways; and (4) affirms the teenager's present qualities but also sets standards for future conduct, using reason as well as power and shaping by regimen and reinforcement to achieve objectives.

The authoritative control, when used by parents, educators, and, in our particular situation, by the group co-therapists, fostered what Baumrind refers to as a particular kind of social competency, which she calls "instrumental competence."

Baumrind sees the authoritarian adult as valuing obedience, in favor of punishment, keeping the child or adolescent in a subordinate role, and restricting autonomy. The authoritarian adult does not encourage verbal give-and-take and may be either overconcerned and protective or may neglect the child or adolescent.

She views the permissive adult as affirmative, accepting, and benign in style toward the child's or adolescent's impulses and actions. The permissive parent is focused on lowering to the lowest level any restraint on the child or adolescent consistent with the youngster's survival. Again, as with the authoritarian adult, the permissive adult may be evading responsibility for the youngster's development through neglect.

The family context, particularly parental style, plays a major role in whether a youngster moves toward social competency or various kinds of antisocial behavior or mental illness or both. Gantman (1978), in examining differences in family-interaction patterns among families with normal, disturbed, and drug-abusing adolescents, found that the normal family was significantly different from the other two groups in frequency of scapegoating of the adolescent and ability to reach a decision.

Other research (Bandura, 1960) focused on the role of family interactions, particularlly how poor parental conflict management can promote aggression in males. Kerfoot (1980) looked at the context of the family in relation to adolescent suicide.

More recently focusing on family research, Nicholi (1985) notes the necessity of a close, warm, sustained relationship with both parents as a hallmark for normal development of children and adolescents. Further, Nicholi comments that in terms of the etiology of nonorganic psychopathology, adults with such disorders have a common history of parental absence, usually because of death, divorce, or a demanding job.

Returning to the task at hand, our working definition of social competency for the adolescents we treat and the model we have developed is the following: A unique set of set-perceptions and interpersonal skills that foster the development of meaningful relationships and the mastery of significant life events, and that move the adolescent toward a level of maturity and healthy self-parenting sufficient to meet the challenges of adulthood.

Our major focus is not on the psychopathology of adolecents, although certain aspects of psychopathology for many of our adolescents are strongly contextual, tied to unhealthy family relationships and patterns, interactions with faulty role models (or the absence of competent adult role models), and failure on the part of the adolescents to move into competent peer relationships by midadolescence.

We found that many of our adolescents had no distinguishable peer relationships, were strongly alienated from their famlies, and were terribly lonely. Others had had disastrous experiences with pseudopeer groups, usually involving drug abuse or other antisocial behavior. From these tragic family and peer group experiences, our adolescents developed symptoms in an effort to deal with the internal and external chaos in their lives. These symptoms were, in many instances, the basis for their hospitalization or incarceration.

Our observations of adolescents in group therapy were consistent with other clinicians' work. Winnicott's (1972) view that "environmental failure" plays a significant role in moving midadolescents toward the need for professional help was certainly evident in our population. Solnit's (1969) position regarding the strong need for adolescents to interact with adults, and Miller's (1973) conclusion that midadolescents experience failure in psychological maturation when they are isolated from adults other than parents, were also borne out in the adolescents we treated in group therapy.

The longer we worked with adolescents in the group, the more we came to view their symptoms as unfortunate survival mechanisms and ultimately self-defeating attempts to deal with dysfunctional family situations and environmental failure. With this understanding, we viewed the adolescent group as a context in which we could provide healthy parenting while simultaneously facilitating the development of meaningful peer relationships, thereby addressing the two major areas of deficit.

It was our primary goal that the adolescents would leave the group therapy experience with the ability to engage in healthy self-parenting and to continue their development of meaningful interpersonal relationships and social competency. In this context, we focus on the healthy part of the adolescent and on the methods we have discovered to be useful in building social competency through our model of group therapy. Finally, it is our hope that some of the principles, strategies, and tactics developed in our group will prove useful to other therapists, as well as to parents, teachers, and community leaders who are involved with adolescents.

THE DEVELOPMENT OF OUR PROGRAM

Many adolescent units within general medical facilities, institutes, state hospitals, and mental health centers are viewed as difficult to operate or tolerate within the larger system; consequently, they receive lower priorities as treatment programs or, in some instances, are closed.

Emotionally disturbed adolescents are often seen as inadequate accommodators to the rules or culture of the larger hospital or clinic. They have a reputation of confronting hospital or clinical authorities more fequently, demanding more activities, eating more food, destroying more property, running away more often, and appearing less appreciative of help than other patients. Thus, mental health administrators are often understandably ambivalent toward the presence of adolescent treatment programs in their facilities.

Our experience is that when key administrators become ambivalent, the ambivalence is frequently mirrored in the clinicians' work at the treatment level. Under these conditions, treatment deteriorates. Adolescent inpatients can sense mixed feelings on the part of a facility, whether on a systemwide, treatment, or caregiver level. Fortunately, in our case, these factors were well reviewed with the Hall Institute administration before the unit opened. This awareness, in combination with a strong training mandate, allowed the unit to begin operation with little administrative ambivalence.

Just as it is crucial for the larger system to support enthusiastically an adolescent unit, it is also important that, within the unit, the staff view group therapy as an important and necessary treatment modality. It is imperative that the positive attitude be communicated directly to the adolescents; otherwise, group therapy could be construed as "playtime." If group therapy is devaluated by the unit staff, attendance problems will develop and other therapies, programs, or administrative issues will take priority over group therapy times.

Because of the popularity of group therapy at the time, it would have been difficult during the early 1970s to think about developing an adolescent inpatient unit without a group psychotherapy program. There is also a common-sense notion that adolescents tend to gather naturally in groups; the development of a formalized therapeutic experience capitalizes on this natural arrangement. Well-adjusted adolescents from healthy families use their peer groups to help them separate from parents and to provide a bridge for the transition into adulthood. Unfortunately, the adolescents in our unit who came to the group psychotherapy program were not separating successfully from their families and, for the most part, had faulty peer group experiences.

Our rationale for the group psychotherapy program, therefore, centered around providing a caring, flexible, therapeutic intervention that would meet the adolescents' developmental needs, overcome skill deficits, and correct maladaptive behaviors. Group therapy would capitalize on the high value that adolescents place on being together in a group and would neutralize, to some degree, the artificiality and awkwardness experienced by the adolescents in their individual psychotherapy. It would also give them a social forum in which to work on family issues at a distance and not become overloaded, as they sometimes felt they were in their actual family therapy work. Finally, it would allow them to experience a "quasi family," in which they could recreate and rework family issues such as authority struggles, parental abuse, or problems with siblings.

The group psychotherapy program offered a social context with peers and competent adult co-therapists, within which members could safely communicate problems. The social context of group therapy allowed some adolescents to experience a healthy peer group for the first time and allowed others to discover the difference between a healthy peer group and a faulty or pseudopeer group.

The group facilitated communication of important themes in normal adolescent development, such as dominance-submission concerns, independence-dependence struggles, gender and sexual identity worries, and educational-vocational anxieties. Many of these themes had not been addressed by the adolescents because of disorganized or pathological family backgrounds or poor peer groups; consequently, the group psychotherapy program offered them an opportunity to do important developmental work. It gave to each member the broadest, most flexible therapy intervention in terms of a social context in which to practice newly acquired, healthier behavior with peers and adults, which would serve them in their movement toward competent adulthood.

The clinical material concerning our adolescent group therapy program comes from several settings: We saw adolescents as inpatients at a youth services correctional institution, as outpatients at a community mental health center, and in an adolescent inpatient unit of the William S. Hall Psychiatric Institute.

The major influence on our conceptualization of adolescent group therapy was the Hall Institute inpatient group, which functioned as a clinical service as well as a forum for training residents and interns in adolescent group therapy. The co-therapists in this group were George Holmes and Lucy Gordon.

Our model of adolescent group therapy is the product of an inpatient adolescent unit that was designed in the 1970s and is quite similar to the adolescent residential treatment center commonly seen today. The patients, male and female, were primarily between the ages of fourteen and eighteen; they were in treatment as inpatients for periods ranging from six to eighteen months. In all the clinical examples of material produced in our group therapy sessions, the identifying patient data (e.g., name and age) have been changed to maintain patient confidentiality.

We used a variety of group structures at different times, often in response to the changing population of the adolescent unit. Over the years we worked with mixed groups as well as groups that were all-female and all-male. We used a variety of co-therapy arrangements and learned a great deal about the relative effectiveness of each and the circumstances under which each might be more or less useful.

For example, in the beginning of the program, the group was to be mixed, with one male therapist and several male and female ward counselors participating as co-therapists. Although this was helpful in terms of the ward staff's investment in and identification with the group therapy program, clinically it was the least effective model. The group was too large, and less verbal adolescents were allowed to face into the woodwork. The ward staff's presence inhibited disclosure, and the group remained superficial. Sessions amounted to little more than ward meetings.

At one point we had one male group and one female group. This model appeared preferable when the inpatient population tended toward early adolescence—ages twelve to fourteen—and worked best with male and female co-therapists. Another time we had one group oriented toward verbal insight and another toward activity, communication , and skill development. This model was used when there was a great diversity within the unit in terms of ages, developmental levels, cognitive functioning, and verbal skills.

While these and other variations were tried, one thing became increasingly clear: Whether the group consisted of all males, all females, or was mixed, the use of a male co-therapist and a female co-therapist working as a team offered the broadest and richest opportunities for therapeutic growth and change. The format that eventually developed was what might be called a verbal, insight-oriented, mixed group, with an emphasis on interpersonal relationships and problem solving.

THE PROCESS OF THE GROUP

The guiding theoretical rationales for our group therapy program came into focus as we struggled through the difficult early years as group therapists. As we experienced the adolescents in the group, we saw that their behavior did not fit into one neat theoretical package. If there was a fluidity of defense mechanisms operating in one member and a rigid defense posture in another, a psychoanalytic perspective was useful in understanding the group members. When we listened to them talk about growing up, a developmental-psychosocial outlook was helpful, particularly when they focused on their normative life crises, the cultural and institutional expectations placed on them, and the dilemmas they faced. Social learning theory enriched our understanding of the impact of poor adult and peer models and how these models negatively affected their socialization processes, especially in interpersonal skills. Finally, existential theory was useful when our adolescents expressed the pain of their alienation, loneliness, and, at times, the meaninglessness of their lives.

The notion from Sullivan (1953) that "adolescence is spontaneously the most therapeutic time in the developmental cycle" helped us to be flexible enough to see the healthy interpersonal aspects of the adolescents and to concentrate on the promotion of interpersonal competency. We drew on concepts from the area of primary prevention such as problem solving, peer consultation, and social skill building as tactics in the promotion of social competency.

In discussing the roles our adolescents developed within the group, we used the Interaction Process Analysis by Bales (1950) as a basic conceptual tool. Our adolescents emerged with roles similar to those observed in adult process groups, ranging from negative socioemotional (disagreeing, showing tension, and antagonism) to positive socioemotional (agreeing, showing tension release, and solidarity). Task-oriented interactions such as raising questions or attempting answers also appeared (asking or giving orientation, suggestions, and opinions).

Our consideration of the roles the adolescents developed led us to reflect on our own leadership styles, the negative and positive leadership styles of the adolescents, the group climate, and the levels of group cohesiveness.

We used another set of group interaction categories developed by Heckel, Holmes, and Rosecrans (1971) from an adult group therapy population to help refine our perceptions of the group roles being assumed by the adolescents at various times. These clinically derived categories included the egocentric participator, the guarded-impersonal environmental commentator, the superficial group interactor, the noncommittal opinion seeker, the therapist-directed environmental commentator, and the occasional opinion seeker. These roles appeared in early group sessions in Heckel's study, as they did in our adolescent group. We saw our adolescents operating as cohesive group builders, superficial environmental commentators, questioning information seekers, radar antenna types, self-oriented verbalizers, and, occasionally, personal-information givers.

In viewing our adolescent group over time, we were sensitive to the theoretical concepts of Whitaker and Lieberman (1964) that there are two major phases in group therapy: a brief formative stage and a more extended established phase. Clinically, we translated this formulation to periods when our group was disorganized compared to some level of organization. We also used Tuckman's (1965) four-stage model of group development, with its emphasis on interpersonal and task functioning of group members, plus the Martin and Hill (1957) framework of six emergent phases of group behavior to examine our adolescent group over time.

When we focused on the group as a whole over an extended period, the most applicable model was a three-stage process in which the group moves from a concentration on environmental issues to working on individual personal problems to a process of generating and working on group themes.

In order to help our group function at higher levels, we developed a set of tactics and strategies that helped us to be more effective, when we encountered resistance, in minimizing regression. We were guided by the principle that one of our major functions was to help develop a secure, caring, trust-filled atmosphere so that challenging, emotionally charged material could be processed in a useful manner. Within the context of our group, we felt a strong responsibility to help the adolescents process important concerns about their past and present problems in order to develop sufficient competency to handle themselves in the future.

After several years of treating inpatient adolescents, certain features emerged (see Table 1). Organizationally, the focus is on content-process issues, interventions at various levels of group development, and changes in group climate.

THE CONTENT OF THE GROUP

In the early stages of our group, the content of the communication was characterized by "environmental comments," which were often unrelated to the adolescents' problems. This was the most difficult and trying period for us. The content was essentially a recapitulation of themes from the ward milieu, such as complaints about staff and cotherapists, disruptive comments, and negative leadership behaviors on the part of the adolescents.

At times we dealt passively with the comments as did group members, and at other times we used a confrontational approach. Both approaches left us feeling stuck in a very primitive social environment in which little therapeutic progress was being made. In essence, we were allowing the worst aspects of the ward milieu and the psychopathology of each adolescent's family to be the dominant forces in the group. The climate reverberated with low levels of security, low challenge, and high mistrust. Very few attempts were made to expose current or past psychological pain or to disclose any significant information of a more personal nature.

In order to get unstuck from the primitive content and process of the early stages, we devised a series of interventions: screening procedures designed to establish a group composition with greater potential for therapeutic work; active directing by the co-therapist to gain a more powerful presence in the group; and a modified fishbowl approach that neutralized some of the acting out and negative leadership behaviors of some group members.

These interventions, along with more clinical experience on our part,

Table 1
Adolescent Group Therapy Process

Early Stages	**Middle Stages**	**Later Stages**
Content:	Content:	Content:
Environmental Comments	Personal Disclosures	Group Responses
Complaining about Staff, Therapist, Group	Adolescent Themes	Sophisticated Themes or Problems
Primitive Resistances	Authority Struggles	Incest, Parenting
Acting Out, Silence	Parents, Teachers, Education	Future
Negative Leadership	Peer Relationship	Capacity for Self-parenting or Competence Operating
	Sex	
Process:	Process:	Process:
Rigid	Experimenting with Different Roles	High Levels of Sensitivity
Controlling	Beginning to Process Group Process	Active Listening
Limiting		Highly Effective and Efficient Group Process
Confrontational		

Passivity Withdrawal Explosive Scapegoating	Less Rigid More Comfort Moderate Flexibility	
Interventions: Modified Fishbowl Disarming Negative Leaders Redistributing Power Screening		Interventions: Entering and Leaving of Group Members and Co-Therapists
Low security, low challenge Episodes of boredom, eruption of chaos Low trust, high mistrust Few personal exposures or disclosures	Moderate security, moderate challenge Fewer stuck periods, regressions Moderate trust, low mistrust Moderate amount of personal exposures, disclosures	High security, high challenge High level of stable growth High level of trust High level of personal disclosures

helped the group move to what we call the middle stage. The content became more focused on adolescent themes and on issues relevant to each adolescent. Authority struggles, particularly with parents and teachers, emerged in numerous sessions. Peer relationships and sexual themes were comfortably generated and effectively managed. The process in the group became less rigid and more flexible, and the adolescents began to be able to "process the process" of the group.

Within the adolescent group, we observed an intensity of affect, fluidity of defenses, and a range of behavior far greater than we had experienced in either individual psychotherapy with teenagers or in adult group psychotherapy. The adolescents pushed us to be interested in them as persons, not as patients, to respect them even when they acted out, and to listen to their psychological suffering without taking it over.

Being able to view our group developmentally helped us grow as clinicians and teachers. Over time, the group continued to function with the characteristics of the middle and later stages, with little evidence of the earlier, more primitive stages.

As the content and process became more synchronized, the climate also changed, with the security level and challenge level increasing substantially. There were very few episodes of feeling stuck or moving backward to the primitive earlier stages. A moderate amount of risk taking developed in terms of personal exposure and disclosure.

Just as we needed a set of interventions to move from the early stage to the middle stage, another set of interventions was designed to move the group to an even higher level of functioning. As our group developed a capacity for new levels of intimacy and stability, we found it became highly sensitized to the issues of termination, change, and loss. Since we were involved in training group therapists, we often had trainees rotating through the group at intervals of four to six months, resulting in frequent terminations. Similarly, when patients terminated and new patients arrived, loss became a powerful group theme.

We found that the higher the level of group functioning, the more powerful the impact of the loss or change. Many of the group members had experienced painful losses that had not been dealt with effectively, and the changes and losses within the group often caused these unresolved issues to reemerge. Although difficult, these situations provided a powerful opportunity for the adolescents to deal with their past and current losses simultaneously and to learn more healthy mechanisms for coping with the end of relationships.

A number of rituals and techniques were developed within the group to help the adolescents in this process and to prevent excessive regression. Group psychotherapy at this stage became a meaningful therapeutic experience for everyone involved. Old themes that had been dealt with superficially at earlier periods in the group's development resurfaced and were processed in greater depth. Members processed the group process, often laughing about their old resistant behaviors. They were openly appreciative of the group and protective of its level of functioning. Old members helped new members move fairly quickly to the group's established level, and only minor regressions occurred.

It seemed that as the adolescents gained increased insight into their past behavior, they were simultaneously experiencing and practicing healthier interactions and relationships in a concrete way within the group. This combination of cognitive and experiential change was particularly powerful at this stage. Through this process, the group members gradually began to give up their previous pathological identities in favor of newer, healthier self-perceptions.

During this phase, the adolescents worked diligently at understanding their own and their parents' behavior, often dealing with the question of why their parents could not parent them more adequately. As they began to understand and accept their parents' strengths and weaknesses, they began to pull out of dysfunctional family patterns and gain a newer and healthier sense of control.

They processed themes of trust, dependence-independence, and sexuality, and began to experiment with increased intimacy within the group. They disclosed increasingly sensitive personal information and received acceptance, feedback, and supportive confrontation from the group and the co-therapists. Some of the most tender moments we have witnessed in our clinical work occurred during this phase. We were struck by their capacity for caring, particularly in light of the emotional pain many of them had endured.

This was the most enjoyable and in many ways the easiest phase of group therapy, despite the intensity of some of the material. As therapists, we felt synchronized with the group members and experienced a strong alliance. Our role became less directive and more facilitative as the group functioned in an increasingly autonomous way. What we were able to give to the group members at this stage was of much greater depth and meaning than what we had been able to offer earlier.

TRAINEES

Throughout our work with the adolescent group, we were involved in supervising trainees assigned to the program. The supervision process proved to be a special learning experience in which we encountered numerous fascinating problems, including passivity on the part of the trainees. Passivity was an issue we dealt with as co-therapists in our earlier group work, but it proved to be a more complex issue for some of the trainees.

We usually supervised two trainees during the group sessions. It soon became apparent that many of the painful aspects of the adolescent group experience were being mirrored by the trainees, which called for the development of specific tactics. We also had to confront the fact that certain trainees were highly effective adolescent group therapists, and others were not. We were impressed by how actively the adolescents would penetrate areas of vulnerability in the trainees, and how this needed to be handled compassionately in supervision.

OVERVIEW

Our book draws on the psychiatric, social work, and physiological literature dealing with adolescent group therapy from research and clinical perspectives. We also relied heavily on our own clinical experience as therapists and as teachers and supervisors.

In order to get a sense of the "why" of group therapy for adolescents, we examine, in chapter 2, the history of adolescent group therapy. Next, we examine the developmental issues and environmental context of our adolescents to see how well our model of group therapy accommodated these factors. Finally, we discuss how the phenomena of natural groupings and the absence of natural groupings play a role in producing dysfunctional or healthy teenagers.

Chapter 3 reviews the numerous issues that deal with group composition. Data from the research literature focus on variables such as single-sex groups, mixed-sex groups, age levels, inpatient versus outpatient status, and other considerations. The data are then contrasted with our clinical experience. For example, we attempt to synthesize what is known from research about selection with clinical and institutional realities facing all practitioners.

In chapter 4 we look at the impact of the physical environment on the group therapy process, again tempering the research findings with our own experience. We also offer suggestions about the most ideal setting for adolescent group therapy.

In chapter 5, we review the many techniques used in adolescent group therapy. The literature provides a variety of approaches to dealing with the problems unique to working with adolescents in group therapy. We give examples of clinical techniques we used but warn against excessive use of them, while at the same time suggesting techniques we feel have the greatest potential for benefiting the adolescent group therapy process.

The group's more stabilized phase of development, in which group members began to increase significantly their self-disclosures, is the focus of chapters 6 and 7. They started to share very personal historical information and to describe how their behavior was changing outside the group—with their families and peers and in individual therapy. The use of the co-therapists' dialogue and tactics for dealing with changes in the makeup of the group are discussed in these two chapters.

The themes and possible curative factors in adolescent group therapy are the focus of chapter 8. The chapter emphasizes the emergence of various themes or content at specific stages. (Certain material and themes are processed more meaningfully at certain phases of the group.) Much of the data comes from our own clinical experience and the reflection and comments of fellow clinicians who work as therapists with adolescent groups.

Chapter 9 looks at the co-therapy relationship. The research literature gives us information about therapists' personalities and styles and some data on adolescent group therapists. We comment about our own experiences and those of fellow clinicians.

In chapter 10 we deal with supervision of trainees and focus on the problems inherent in helping clinicians become skilled adolescent group therapists. We use the research and our own clinical work to draw conclusions that might be helpful to other clinicians in their roles as teachers and supervisors.

We use chapter 11 to sum up and make recommendations about adolescent group therapy. We also discuss the tragic environmental contexts and detrimental interpersonal relationships that damage many adolescents in the critical stage of their development. Out of this concern, we have postulated a series of primary prevention interventions based on our model of adolescent group therapy, which should help prevent some of the psychopathology seen in our clinical settings.

2

WHY GROUP THERAPY FOR ADOLESCENTS?

> Just because the message may never be received does not mean it is not worth sending.
>
> —Segaki
> David Stackton, trans.

In this chapter we examine the roots of group therapy in the literature and then focus on some of the important events and persons associated with the development of adolescent group therapy. Next, we turn to attachment theory to give us a much broader and in-depth understanding of the deficits and maladaptive behavior we saw in our adolescent group.

GROUP PSYCHOTHERAPY HISTORICAL PERSPECTIVES

Many authors have described adolescence as the time "in between" childhood and adulthood. While to some degree adolescent group therapy has its own history as a treatment modality, it has grown "up" as a continuation of group work with children and "down" from the rich history of adult group psychotherapy. What has emerged is in every sense unique.

The rules that govern or describe the behavior of children and adults do not adequately address the behaviors of adolescents. Therapists working with adolescents soon learn to form new guidelines for therapy and new goals relevant only to this age group.

In many instances, group psychotherapy is considered as having its origins in work with adults rather than children or adolescents. Mullan and Rosenbaum (1953) and Rosenbaum and Berger (1963) claim that Joseph Hersey Pratt, an internist practicing in Boston at the beginning of the twentieth century, was the founder of group psychotherapy. They note that in 1905, Pratt was treating tubercular patients who had become disheartened about their difficulties in handling the social and medical aspects of their disease. They indicate that Pratt's groups of twenty-five adult patients met in a class-type setting and that the meetings were mainly educational, with the goal of raising the hopes of the participants.

Moving to the European scene, Mullan and Rosenbaum and Rosenbaum and Berger report that concurrent with Pratt's work in America, a European, J. L. Moreno, was working with children, displaced persons, and prostitutes. The authors indicate that Moreno felt strongly that his work and Pratt's class method were starting points of group psychotherapy. Further, they reveal that in Germany and Austria during the 1920s through the 1950s, "collective counseling" was being used to treat alcoholics, persons who stammered, persons suffering from sexual difficulties, and neurotics.

It appears that the earliest underpinning for the development of adult group therapy in this century centered on the need to treat portions of the population who were stigmatized or socially rejected. The early methods of group psychotherapy had an educational component and the goal of helping members to be more hopeful.

Freud's earliest writing reflected his orientation toward an intrapsychic theory of human behavior and individualized treatment in psychoanalysis. In writing about group psychology, Freud (1948) indicated that the group leader is, in effect, the primal father. The group seeks to be led by this powerful force and typically displays a strong need for authority.

While most psychoanalysts and psychoanalytically-oriented psychiatrists did not move toward the group modality of treatment during the first half of the twentieth century, a few ventured into group work. Marsh (1935), a psychiatrist, followed Pratt's inspirational approach while working with adult psychiatric patients; Wender (1936) used psychoanalytic concepts in dealing with borderline psychotics in groups in a state hospital; and Schilder (1939) worked with fifty people in outpatient group treatment using psychoanalytic concepts.

DEVELOPMENT OF ADOLESCENT GROUP THERAPY

Turning to adolescent group therapy, we focus on the paper by Rachman and Raubolt (1984) based on the latter's dissertation. The paper examines the impact specific individuals had on the early use of adolescent group psychotherapy. A critically important aspect of the Rachman and Raubolt paper deals with the notion that the pioneers in adolescent group therapy had no communication with each other and no theory of adolescent development as a guiding framework.

The authors write that the clinicians involved with adolescents in group treatment were August Aichhorn, Fritz Redl, and S. R. Slavson. Although Betty Gabriel and Kenneth Wollan were important innovators who worked in groups with adolescents, they were forgotten in terms of their contributions.

Rachman and Raubolt credit Moreno as possibly having the first contact with an adolescent group; however this was probably reported as or associated with adult group therapy. They credit Alfred Adler and his associates with the first group therapy approach with adolescents, noting that it had certain limitations because of the strong role played by adult group members in terms of adult self-disclosures, advice, direct suggestion, and problem solving, and the lack of available interaction between peers on personal difficulties.

The authors see Aichhorn as the first adolescent group psychotherapist. A former teacher and a disciple of Anna Freud, he applied psychoanalytic principles to the education or reeducation of ''delinquent, dissocial, and problem children'' in the 1920s. Aichhorn and a colleague developed a method of categorizing the intellectual and social characteristics of their adolescent patients in order to achieve the most beneficial group composition for treatment. One group of aggressive youngsters seen by Aichhorn in the 1930s appears to be the first documented adolescent therapy group (Aichhorn, 1935, 1964). Much of his approach, as described in *Wayward Youth* (1935), takes a broad perspective and marks the first use of a therapeutic community in which all activities were scrutinized and made part of the treatment process.

Other interesting developments in group therapy also took place in the 1930s. Slavson (1934) did important pioneer work by using a group method for the diagnosis and treatment of children with behavioral problems at the Jewish Board of Guardians in New York. Bender and Schilder (1937) established group activities for patients on a children's ward as a method of psychotherapy.

Slavson (1943) was clearly a major proponent of using group psychotherapy for adolescents. In his later writing (1958) he indicated that adolescents coming to therapy could not be helped by a guidance or counseling approach alone, but needed a group method, which he termed ''para-analytic.'' He saw the greatest differences beween purely analytic adult group psychotherapy and para-analytic group therapy as being related to the activity level or participation of the therapist. He viewed the therapist in the para-analytic group with adolescents as much more active in leading, and at times directing, the sessions.

Ginnott (1958) was another strong proponent of active and flexible methods of group therapy with children and adolescents. The important observations by Slavson and Ginnott concerning the activity level of the therapist proved to be invaluable in the evolution and teaching of our model of adolescent group psychotherapy.

After World War II, psychiatric inpatients and outpatients in veterans hospitals were treated using group psychotherapy, often as the primary treatment modality. In the 1950s, there was an explosion in the clinical and research literature on group psychotherapy, group dynamics, and training groups. In the 1960s, after the passage of the Comprehensive Community Mental Health and Retardation Act, there was further popularization of group psychotherapy, as mental health services were made available to larger portions of the general population.

During the late 1960s and early 1970s interest in groups was expanded by the human-potential movement, with its emphasis on group relations, encounter groups, and community living. The article by Schwartzberg, Mullens, and Groce (1971) suggests that as the increased demand surfaced for mental health services at all levels, professional manpower used group diagnostic and psychotherapy approaches more and more extensively.

It was also during this period that increasing numbers of adolescents were seen professionally for adjustment problems or emotional illness. Delinquent adolescents incarcerated for criminal behavior received group therapy as part of their treatment or rehabilitation program. MacLennan and Felsenfeld (1968) authored the first book to focus on the special dilemmas of group psychotherapy with adolescents. *Group Counseling and Psychotherapy with Adolescents* made a strong statement: in order to help adolescents in group psychotherapy, the therapist must understand the role that dysfunctional social systems play in the dysfunction of individuals, especially the adolescent.

Later, Berkovitz (1972) edited a volume, *Adolescents Grow in Groups: Experiences in Adolescent Group Psychotherapy*, which essentially described the psychotherapeutic experiences of thirty professionals working with adolescents in group therapy.

And finally, Sugar (1975) was the editor of a classic book, *The Adolescent in Group and Family Therapy*, in which leading psychotherapists described specific uses of group or family therapy with adolescents. These three volumes certainly indicate that adolescent group therapy as a treatment modality has a well-established identity, which we hope can be enriched by our contribution.

The group dynamics movement developed by Kurt Lewin and his students and associates, particularly Jerome Frank, Lee Bradford, Henry Reicken, Dorwin Cartwright, Alvin Zander, Warren Bennis, Kenneth Benne, Murray Horwitz, and others, made a considerable impact on our conceptual system for group psychotherapy. Their practical applications and research provided a starting place for our therapeutic model with its focus on the individual in a social context and the importance of the experiential field in developing and maintaining the undesired behaviors. But the contributions of this group have been most significant in their ability to examine group behavior as a process that can be measured, evaluated, and modified. Those contributions that most significantly affected our approach are

1. Lewin's concept of a cultural island as a method for helping people unfreeze from traditional behaviors, which is a strong justification for the inpatient adolescent in group psychology and the therapeutic community provided in enlightened treatment settings.
2. Lewin's adoption of Wiener's concept of feedback for behavioral purposes. Rather than setting a disruptive or negative value to it, he saw it as a means of providing group members with data of which they were unaware or to which they had limited access.
3. The conceptual framework of the group as a system.

It remains for the attachment researchers to provide us with a working and experimentally based theory of what can go wrong in the early developmental years, and where the focus of a change system could be placed.

THE ADOLESCENT SELF

As therapists, we accept the proposition that the basic adolescent self we deal with in psychotherapy arose as a result of interactions with caregivers who formed the adolescent's early experience base. This self consists of attitudes, expectations, and feelings that emerge from the triadic and dyadic interactions with the primary caregivers.

Regardless of quality—consistent, inconsistent, or even absent—a matrix, or organizational pattern, is formed. Eventually, this becomes a social phenomenon, in which the qualities of the emergent self are embedded in the interaction process. Thus, as Ainsworth et al. (1978) indicate, the nature of the caregiving environment is all-important and, to the extent that it is "alert and responsive" to the newborn's reflex signals, patterns of expectations for responses to needs are formed, self issues are formed, and, even more important, the basis for reactivity and responding, initially in the dyad or triad, sets the course for all subsequent interactions.

Hartup (1989) makes the point that initially attachments form in two directions: vertically to individuals of greater knowledge or social power, and horizontally with individuals who have similar degrees of social power. Most vertical attachments are with parents, adult caregivers, or older siblings and frequently involve nurturing and control on the part of the older person and "submission and succorance" from the child. Horizontal relationships, at least over time, are marked by reciprocity and expectation of equality.

In successful vertical relationships, children receive security and protection for the extended period of dependency until they move to functioning on their own. This is the training ground for social skills through modeling and behavioral shaping. Deficits and defective learning at this stage provide the child with faulty tools for social interaction, leading to problems later in horizontal relationships. Vertical relationships emerge in the first year, whereas horizontal relationships become most visible by the third year.

Negative horizontal relationships involve the inability to engage in reciprocity and a failure to make a commitment to others of relative equality. Children who experience attachment deficits are unable to engage in the usual behaviors that are basic to social interaction and friendships such as loyalty, self-disclosure, and mutual understanding. These friendships are typically same-sex and are qualitatively different from the child's interactions with caregivers.

Of greatest concern to us are the disturbed or troubled children who are brought to treatment. Achenbach and Edelbrock (1981) report that depending on age, 30 to 75 percent of children seen in child guidance clinics have disturbances in their peer relationships; this is on the order of twice as many as for nonreferred children. These children, as with our adolescents, had fewer friends and interpersonal contacts, less stable relationships, and poorer understanding of appropriate social interactions. Often rejected by others, many referred children seek out others with backgrounds similar to their own, forming dissident groups or cliques. By adolescence, these deficits are well established and difficult to modify. Adolescents confront others with fixed expectations, operating as if these expectations are legitimate.

But to argue that all adolescent emotional difficulties arise from traumatic family relationships represents the greatest oversimplification. It ignores cause and effect, innate or hereditary versus learned behavior, temporal sequencing, the family system, and disruptive changes that may alter the field of individual perceptions. Additionally, there are natural catastrophic events, such as relocations or school changes; their consequences have been extensively described in the literature.

It is our purpose in speaking of developmental issues to provide both documentary and clinical evidence in support of our contention that events in the family during infancy and childhood determine whether or not one will reach adolescence as a mentally healthy individual. This has been the position of practitioners since it was first formulated by Freud, but with little other than clinical judgment presented as evidence. Rutter (1985) and Bowlby (1988) provide excellent summary statements relating to retrospective, prospective, and ethological data supporting the role of dysfunctional familial behaviors in producing adolescent maladaptive responses in the bio-psycho-social areas.

We share with Bowlby the belief that, while genetic factors may significantly contribute both to personality development and to psychopathology, the impact of the environment in its many forms has an enormous influence on observed behaviors. These behaviors are now the major focus of researchers. Our position is to recognize genetic limitations and predispositions in behavior, but we feel the evidence points clearly to an environmental shaping of observable behavior patterns.

Harlow's work with nonhuman primates (once thought to be prisoners of their genetic codes) establishes the vital role social learning plays in the development of behavior even at this level. Isolation or inadequate nurturing during early development produced dramatic deficits in the maternal and sexual behavior of the monkeys reared under these conditions (Harlow, 1958).

In working with adolescents, clinicians are constantly confronted by the relationship between present mental state and a knowledge of an individual's intimate personal relationships, whether they are or have been warm, supportive, and harmonious or angry, tense, anxious, emotionally distant, or even totally absent.

While there is general agreement as to causality, there exist few conceptual frameworks by which to document supporting research and theory. Instead, the field has been replete with psychological and psychiatric jargon, descriptive terms and labels that add little in the way of explanation, cause, or effect. From our perspective, the work on attachment theory—especially the efforts of Bowlby, Rutter, Waters, Ainsworth, Sroufe, and others—provides us with growing support for the role of the family and its parenting skills in producing the dysfunctional behaviors in our adolescent group members.

As indicated by Rutter (1985), supportive research on attachment theory has gone through a series of phases. The first of these concerns the effectual components of mothering in infancy. The second involves conceptualization of different types of life experiences from the standpoint of loss or threat (separation, coercion, delinquency risk) in infancy and childhood and their impact on later behavior, especially from the position of risk potential. Further, there has been a focus on experiences vital to potential development and those behaviors that differ markedly from this ideal.

A third and current phase of research is related to what we would call a hardiness dimension (Kobasa, 1979). Rutter (1985) states that it is unusual for more than half of the children exposed to extreme stress and adversity to become emotionally disturbed. Similarly, some adults, following stress or disturbing life events, show an increase in depression, but most do not.

Early explanations advanced to explain the survival of traumatic events involved a postulation of genetically determined invulnerability in some children (Anthony, 1968). This idea has been effectively challenged by a number of writers (Garmezy & Masten, 1986), with the emergent model suggesting that there is a ''relative concept of resilience'' rather than a more absolute model of invulnerability (Rutter, 1985).

As practicing clinicians, we have often sought the caregiver, whether a grandparent, a sibling, or another, who provided emotional support to a client who should be more dysfunctional or disturbed based on family dynamics. In virtually every instance, our search revealed a significant caregiver who served in place of the dysfunctional parent.

Another popular model involves the examination of differences in vulnerability that increase an individual's susceptibility to stress. These stresses may be increased or diminished by the buffering effects of social supports. Unfortunately, the issue is highly complex, and the instruments of assessment are still being developed; findings are at times contradictory and inconsistent.

This is especially true when examining familial and peer roles in reducing the effects of stress. Many factors contain both negative and positive aspects. For example, peers may provide emotional support, yet prove to be emotionally demanding and stress producing. And while individuals may list a variety of social supports and indicate frequent contact, the degree of effectiveness of these contacts is not easily assessed.

Rutter (1985) mentions another model, used frequently in research in which the researchers attempt to develop meaning by adding negative factors and offsetting that by the effects of positive life experiences. These have some promise, but, as in the authors' research, it is not possible to assess the precise processes under which risk factors and positive experiences operate, how they interact, and what their contributions are to individual differences in vulnerability or risk. When applying these factors to adolescents, with their limited experience base and differences in establishing causal relationships, the problems are even greater.

Most of the adolescents dealt with in our treatment programs, inpatient or outpatient, reflect areas of vulnerability, and all lack, to some degree, the protective factors encountered in optimal or normal development.

Table 2, reflecting salient developmental issues provided by Sroufe (1979), combines the important elements from the formulations of Erik-

Table 2
Salient Development Issues

Age (Years)	Issues
0 - 1	Biological regulation; harmonious dyadic interaction; formation of effective attachment relationships
1 - 2½	Exploration, experimentation, and mastery of the object world (caregiver as secure base); individuation and autonomy; responding to external control of impulses
3 - 5	Flexibility, self-control; self-reliance; initiative; identification and gender concept; establishing effective peer contacts (empathy)
6 - 12	Social understanding (equity, fairness); gender constancy; same-sex chumships; sense of "industry" (competence); school adjustment
13+	"Formal operations" (flexible perspective taking, "as if" thinking); loyal friendships (same sex); beginning heterosexual relationships; emancipation; identity

son (1963) and Piaget (1969) with the linking of their formulations as provided in the work of Rutter (1981) and Rutter, Quinton, and Liddle (1983). Working from this model of normal or optimal development, Rutter has described seven ways in which failing to achieve the age landmarks (failures to adapt) results in emotional disorder. (1) Experience leads to disorder at the time, which then persists; (2) experience leads to bodily changes that influence later functioning; and (3) there are altered patterns of behavior at the time, which only later take the form of disorder.

Others are less direct: (4) early events may change the family circumstances, in time producing disorder; (5) sensitivities to stress or coping styles are modified, later predisposing the person to disorder (or buffering the person against stress); (6) experiences alter the person's self-concept of attitudes, which, in turn, influence the response to later situations; and (7) experience influences behavior through effects on the selection of environments or on the opening up or closing down of opportunities.

Inspection of the items in Table 2 reveals a broadly conceptualized model that includes affective, cognitive, and social areas. Each level requires extensive and complex levels of adaptation involving attachment to the caregivers and their particular qualities, an orientation toward peers, and the requisite styles of the environment.

Each of these complex interactions may have properties that provide for successful adaptation at one level but may impede later adjustment. For instance, overcontrol because of fear of parental reprisal at ages three to five may reduce the child's potential for social interaction and friendship development in early adolescence.

AFFECTIONAL BONDS

Of particular importance in our consideration of attachment is an examination of affectional bonds. Although these bonds in friendship and peer relationships may be flexible, interchangeable, and even replaceable, the significant attachment is a long-lived tie in which the individual is unique, important, and never fully replaceable. Typically, this primary figure is mother, father, or both; in many cases it may be grandparents, older siblings, stepparents, or a high-contact caregiver, such as a nursemaid.

In examining the pathological patterns of attachment, Bowlby (1977), Bretherton (1985), and Paterson and Moran (1988) have indicated that when there has been an extended disruption in the continuity of caregiving, a series of behaviors results. First, crying and other attention demands occur. If the caregiver does not respond, despair follows, with little hope of the caregiver's return. Depression and inactivity are the main presenting behaviors, punctuated occasionally by rage.

The next phase involves apparent forgetting and detachment to the degree that upon the caregiver's eventual return, the child may show avoidance behaviors. This undergoes rapid changes, as anxiety, clinging, and anger toward the caregiver are displayed.

The absence that promotes these behaviors may not always be a physical absence. Threats of the withdrawal of caring or love, and fear of abandonment, may create a sufficient level of anxiety for the development of "anxious" attachment.

Fear of losing the primary caregiver results in high levels of anger, which is repressed because of its destructive potential. As a result, the anger is often displaced on others, and the resulting behavior pattern (Paterson and Moran) is later seen in the DSM III-R classification of borderline personality and dependent personality disorders. As adolescents, persons with these dynamics draw much attention because of their lability and unpredictability.

In "compulsive self-reliance" (Bowlby, 1977), an apparent conclusion has been drawn that there will never be an adequate caregiver available and that the infant/child can rely on no one but himself or herself. This is not volitional but is forced by a fear of attachments and their consequences. As adolescents and adults, such persons do not enter and explore relationships. Instead, they avoid them and are similar to the DSM III-R diagnoses of schizoid and avoidant personality disorders (Paterson and Moran).

A further source of adjustment difficulty arising from flawed attachment that is described by Sroufe et al. (1985) speculated that mothers who are seductive with sons apparently learned that their needs could not be fully met by adults. Sroufe empirically confirmed that these mothers reported personal histories of parental emotional exploitation that included, but was not limited to, incest. Other necessary dynamics were the mother's own mother's distance from her and alienation between her parents, resulting in the father's unmet needs and his turning to her to meet those needs.

It follows that these mothers recapitulate in their behavior a hostility toward daughters and establish the whole negative family configuration, with marked distance from their husbands, thus putting their daughters at risk of exploitation.

These patterns, extended to school age, and more nearly approaching our target population, reveal a common pattern found in adolescent therapy groups: the sexually preoccupied females who seek to validate themselves through sexual interactions, and the males who reject the heterosexual role.

Bowlby (1977) suggests an additional response that occurs as the result of anxious attachment but is rarely seen clinically, at least during adolescence. This is the compulsive caregiver, who denies personal needs and works endlessly to fulfill the needs of others. Such persons are typically long-suffering and self-sacrificing. Even the victims of abuse have convinced themselves that had they done more for the other person, the abuse might not have occurred. In adolescence the manifestation is less clear, though in some instances individuals who appear stable may abandon family, friends, and personal goals and become involved in criminal behavior, not for personal gain but to please a significant other.

If no meaningful attachment is available to the child, the developmental course closely approximates the descriptions given by Spitz (1945) of an institutional population of infants who lacked adequate caregiving. They wasted away, became lethargic, and in some instances died from what he labeled *mirasmus,* a lack of adequate nurturing. Those who survived lacked a capacity for closeness and intimacy and were seen as poorly adjusted loners. Those findings, challenged by others, have gained new empirical support with the research on attachment.

Most significant in today's world of high mobility, high divorce rates, working couples, extrafamilial childcare, latchkey children, and babysitters are problems of the totally absent or lost parent. Occasionally this occurs through death, but most often it is due to divorce. The child's response to parental loss has been best described by Bowlby and Parkes (1970) as consisting of four stages, of varying time spans.

The first and briefest is a dulling of affect, or numbness. This may be punctuated by occasional outbursts of anger or signs of anxiety. In stage two, there is a longing and searching for the lost figure. Some of the behaviors are on an "as if" basis, as if the person were still alive or would soon appear. On one child's chart there were hallucinatory experiences early in this mourning process that continued intermittently for several days.

The third stage is one of despair and disorganization. There is a major disruption in activities and activity levels. Apathy and noninvolvement mark much of the behavior of this phase. Toys may be abandoned, pets ignored (some pets are victims of abuse in the first two stages), and interaction with adult caregivers is passive. Should the child fail to move beyond this phase and reintegrate with the world in the fourth phase, filling the void with new activities and excluding those that had involved the lost person, the result in adolescence appears to be the loner, the compulsively self-reliant child.

In examining replaceable or interchangeable attachments, consider situational events such as a child or adolescent wishing to engage in shooting hoops, attending a movie, or simply hanging out. The child/adolescent will draw on a series of others with whom he or she has affectional bonds. If one friend chooses not to participate, another will be called, and another, until the activity is carried out or abandoned. The activity is central, not the peers, who are essentially interchangeable.

If, however, the need for affiliation is central and the activity is only presented as a reason for the social interaction, the actors become the focus. If the target person refuses to participate, the activity is changed or dropped. In adolescent group psychotherapy we typically encounter both the activity and the affiliation as irreplaceable by the group members, or, conversely, they deny any need for intimacy, at least in early stages of group development.

As to the level of need becomes more critical and the issues relate to security, companionship, nurturing, assistance, guidance, or dealing with issues of competence and self-worth, the range of actors who can meet these needs diminishes greatly and they may fall to a primary caregiver or others to whom the child/adolescent is attached. If there are perceived deficits in meeting these attachment needs, either real or imagined, the child/adolescent is seen to be at risk. Some or all of these issues are present in each group member.

Research in learning tells us that 100 percent reinforcement is neither necessary nor desirable for optimum growth and development. Rather, the expectation that a particular attachment need will usually or eventually be met typically results in the desired and approved response to the caregiver or the person with whom the affectional bond exists, a feeling of "if not now, they will be there for me, and my needs will be met."

In most instances, therapy involves a reframing or reexamination of both experiences and persons in order to meet needs and modify situations more effectively, not simply for the client, but for the whole family unit. One of the developmental tasks to be provided by effective psychotherapy is the replacement of defective attachment models with those more able to deal with the six expressed needs.

NATURAL GROUPINGS

Once the child leaves the protective environment of the home there is a constant demand to participate in the natural groups in the environment. Although some are partially interactive and structured, such as school- or church-related participation, most other settings demand a continuous interaction by the child. These interactions outside the home, begin in preschool and kindergarten, moving to the block, the neighborhood, the unsupervised playground, and later at parties and in other social activities for which time and place are specified. Social interaction, however, is left to the individual.

It is in these contexts that the effects of early learning, those related to both vertical and horizontal attachment problems, become highly manifest. Parents, who have their own experiential base and are influenced by a flood of popular literature underscoring what should be appropriate adolescent behavior, often inappropriately and intermittently apply these ideas to their child or adolescent. Unfortunately, the real issues facing the family are rarely addressed.

The natural groups of greatest influence are the family, the gang (social group), the school, the block, the neighborhood, and the church, in descending order. Their importance is in part relative to the time spent by the adolescent in each context during the formative years, or until the child reaches the treatment facility.

We have already explored the symptoms and problems arising from defects in attachment, but we have barely touched on the parameters of the social milieu in which the adolescent operates, and the flaws and defects that occur there. Sroufe (1979) provides insight into what may occur in interactions between two insecurely attached persons, but we need to explore extensively the social context in which they operate in their environment. When applied to the psychotherapeutic setting, the social context is often a family model, with the co-therapists operating as parent surrogates, at least in the initial perceptions of the group members.

Frequently, adolescents referred for treatment are operating from a social deficit model—lack of social supports, inadequate social shelters, shyness, egocentricity, low self-esteem and self-worth, limited experience—which results in inappropriate responses, and gender and role problems, to name a few. Further issues involve the dependency-independency struggle, the work of peer interaction and acceptance, and sexuality.

These, in our experience, are the major issues dealt with most successfully in psychotherapy in adolescent groups. They are all problems of social interaction and, as a result, are best dealt with in a multidimensional model of feedback, problem solving, and support available only in groups.

SUMMARY

In this chapter we have attempted to provide a sense of how we arrived at our approach to adolescent group psychotherapy. We have discussed the work of therapists who have influenced our thinking, either through our acceptance of their ideas, or through the challenges they have presented us.

We have also provided our view of the significant theoretical bases for the behavior we have dealt with in our groups. The most exciting of these have been the work of Bowlby, Rutter, Ainsworth, and Sroufe, although many others have enhanced their views and advanced developmental theory. The promise of attachment theory is not merely a causal explanation. In its rigorous search for cause, it has provided a clear identification of deficits, behaviors in need of change, and a classification of those areas that become the work of the group's co-therapists.

3

SELECTED VARIETIES OF THERAPY

Youth, even in its sorrows, has a brilliance of its own.

—Victor Hugo
Les Misérables

In this chapter we are interested in examining a few of the various approaches to adolescent group therapy found in the literature. We also describe in some detail the design of our adolescent group, emphasizing administrative support, screening, and group composition.

VOLUNTEERS IN ADOLESCENT GROUP THERAPY

An innovative approach to adolescent group therapy was initiated by Fine et al. (1977), who used three volunteer nonpatient adolescents in a group therapy program that lasted ten months. Over the course of the program, fifteen adolescents attended five or more sessions. While the youngest and oldest patients appeared to benefit least from the group therapy, other patients, in varying degrees, modeled their behavior on that of the volunteers.

This innovation has been refined to include training for the volunteers before they join the group, and care has been taken to ensure that there are volunteers who are the same age or older than the patients.

Another innovative approach using volunteers was reported by Saffer (1986), who met with a group of young people suffering from the suicide of a friend. The intervention focused on the group's discussion of the feelings engendered by the suicide. The members were all friends of the suicide victims and all volunteered to attend three sessions after being invited. There was no pressure on the members to participate in the group in a particular way. The first session focused on the shock they had experienced and the problems they had comprehending the act. There was no discussion of sadness or loss at this point. They made some attempt to understand the victim's schizophrenic condition; however, they expressed considerable anger about the victim's "aloof isolation" and their own feelings of guilt about whether they were the cause of the suicide. In the final session, the members began to see the suicide in both cognitive and emotional terms.

SEX OFFENDERS, THE SEXUALLY ABUSED, AND SINGLE-SEX GROUPS

Smets and Cebula (1987) developed a group therapy program for adolescent sex offenders after individual therapy proved ineffective. The boys in the program ranged in age from thirteen to eighteen and all had been charged with sexual assault of minors. All the boys in the group were ordered to attend by the court. Those referred to the group who were psychotic, severely learning-disabled, or of borderline intelligence were excluded from the program.

The program was based on five steps, and the boys were told that the group would not end until everyone had completed Level 5. The levels were as follows:

Level 0: I am not saying anything and will not cooperate.

Level 1: I can say why I am here (what the charges were against me) and I am also willing to cooperate.

Level 2: I have shown that I want to cooperate by contributing without having been asked. I also helped others join and participate.

Level 3. I am now ready to tell about the details of what I did to assault a minor. I will tell about whom I did it to, what led up to it, and exactly what happened.

Level 4: I can talk about my own sexuality, the good part and the bad. I have learned to feel OK about discussing sex. I also opened up about having been a victim myself. There are no more secrets.

Level 5: I have made a plan to deal with my victim and my perpetrator. I know how to deal with my sexual desires in the future. I have also received a vote of confidence from the group members.

The therapists used a guilt and shame list as an introduction to Level 3. At Level 4, each adolescent presented his sexual history, using guidelines developed by the therapists. Finally, each group member was required to write a letter about his reactions to the group and mail the letter to the therapist.

The program has apparently had great success; only one of the twenty-one participants has repeated his offense. A key element in the success was the use of a team of a male and a female co-therapist. Having a strong, competent female co-therapist talk directly about sexual issues and sex roles had a major positive effect on the group members.

Hazzard, King, and Webb (1986) reported clinical guidelines for conducting group therapy with sexually abused adolescents. Her population of eleven sexually abused females was self-selected from an initial sample of fifty-five sexually abused females seen in the emergency room of a large metropolitan hospital. All were from low- to middle-income families and eight were black. The types of abuse ranged from rape by a stranger to ongoing incest with an adult male family member.

The group ran for three weeks. The first short-term issues that emerged centered around concern about the emotional reactions of others to the disclosure of sexual abuse, fears that the judge and others would not believe them, and emotional reactions such as anxiety, anger, depression, and guilt. The longer-term issues focused on family relationships. Mother-daughter conflicts were seen in both the rape and incest victims. Other long-term issues faced by the group members were distrust in interpersonal relationships, future sexual adjustment, self-esteem, and self-assertion.

The female therapist conducting the group has offered pragmatic guidelines for therapy with sexually abused adolescent females. She suggests that (1) the group should be scheduled for late afternoon or early evening to minimize disruption of school and work activities; (2) a group with two female co-therapists is the best model for the initial group experience; (3) members should be between eleven and eighteen and should not be severely disturbed or limited intellectually; (4) the group should be open-ended and last for two to six months; (5) there should be a snack time before the group starts; and (6) family cooperation should be maximized in order to minimize sabotage.

In the sessions, the therapist used structured exercises to decrease anxiety and initiate communication about personal issues. Role playing was used to prepare for court appearances or to express feelings to family members. Films provided information about sexuality and decision making.

Golden and Dominak (1986) described their experience in forming and conducting a unique psychotherapy group with severely disturbed female adolescents in a long-term, psychotherapeutically oriented, mixed-sex inpatient unit over a period of twenty-seven months. The rationale for the single-sex group was that the females in the unit were actively seeking support, advice, and feedback about intimacy in relationships with males, birth control, menstruation, and body image. As a result of these concerns, the "women's group" was formed.

The group was composed of severely disturbed female inpatients ranging in age from thirteen to twenty. Two female co-therapists who were in the ward milieu as a psychiatric assistant and a psychiatric nurse ran the group. All female patients in the unit automatically were members of the group, and no one was excluded.

The group focused largely on interpersonal and interactive phenomena; however, patients were encouraged to share relevant past events and relationships that were developmentally significant. The themes in the group included struggles toward separation and individuation from mothers, establishing a sexual identity, and conflicts with intimacy—powerful issues shared by all members and most consistently manifested in the group.

This particular group was instrumental in facilitating a special sense of belonging and creating a union around a set of themes and tasks. The group was also beneficial to the unit in supporting the norms, values, and goals of the psychotherapeutically oriented milieu.

THE WARD GROUP AND THE HUB GROUP

Klein, Brown, and Hunter (1986) developed the ward group, a modified version of traditional group therapy to be used in conjunction with comprehensive long-term treatment for severely ill adolescents and young adults. From a developmental perspective, the ward group closely resembles a family in that it simultaneously pursues diverse, complex, and what may appear at times to be contradictory tasks, such as administrative decision making and traditional group psychotherapy.

The ward group consisted of a number of small groups within a long-term, sixty-bed, psychoanalytically oriented inpatient hospital. The patients, most of them teenagers, were severely disturbed and usually remained in the hospital for more than four hundred days. They met for forty-five- to fifty-minute sessions three times a week, and attendance was mandatory.

Having the ward group so clearly embedded in the various units, however, created boundary issues for the group leaders. Membership, confidentiality, and space and time boundaries had to be demarcated early in the life of the group. Because the ward group functioned at times as an administrative unit and at other times as a therapy group, more complex boundary issues also emerged.

The ward group serves in the context within which patients are able, among other things, to review and negotiate individual statuses and limits, plan group activities and outings, examine the nature and quality of interpersonal relationships that unfold and develop within the group, and begin to comprehend the implications of being a citizen of the group.

Beitel et al. (1983) developed the Hub Group as an innovative approach to group therapy in a short-term inpatient adolescent unit. The Hub Group concept involved a twice-weekly group therapy program organized by wards. The rationale for the Hub Group was the unit staff's recognition of a need for ward-based groups to counteract problems that typically occur among inpatients, such as isolation, lack of positive peer interaction, and ineffective group problem-solving skills. Another goal was to increase the therapeutic involvement of milieu staff.

The hub of a wheel seemed an appropriate metaphor when naming the group therapy program. Central to the Hub Group is a set of contracts, each of which serves as a narrative description of the adolescent's self-image, patterns of relating to others, and methods of handling life experiences. Essentially, it is a treatment plan for the group, developed with the patient's cooperation.

Each contract centers around two labels—one positive and one negative—which symbolize a constellation of behaviors or characteristics and attempt to capture the adolescent's broad personality style. For example, a contract for Laura, an older adolescent, used the images "Lofty Rattlesnake" versus "Blue Ribbon Horse."

At the end of each session, the patients were asked to rate themselves, and to review their performances in the group and determine which image they were most like. If they were most like their positive image, they rated themselves a three; if they were most like their negative image, they rated themselves a one; and if they were some of both, they got a two.

There was a dramatic decrease in the difference between the self-rating and leader rating of patients the longer the group met. In some groups the rating system was abandoned altogether when high levels of cohesiveness were reached.

The Hub Group fosters nurturance and tolerance of others very quickly. The themes of acceptance, attachment, and separation were ever-present despite rapid turnover. The designers of the concept reflected that staff leadership in the groups, whether supportive or confrontational, must always be active.

ADMINISTRATIVE SUPPORT

Administrative support is extremely important to the development and successful functioning of any adolescent treatment program. Our adolescent group therapy program was developed as part of the newly established adolescent inpatient unit of the Child and Adolescent Psychiatric Service of the William S. Hall Psychiatric Institute in Columbia, South Carolina.

The unit was designed primarily to provide inpatient services for an adolescent patient population that was underserved in the early 1970s. It was also meant to offer a wide range of training possibilities for child and adolescent mental health professionals. A mandate from the Institute Planning Committee for high-quality service and training helped secure a strong administrative staff for the creation of the adolescent unit, and, consequently, for its various therapy programs.

SCREENING AND GROUP COMPOSITION

Our early experience in group therapy made it clear that screening and prior contact with the potential group members would be important to the functioning of the group. Initially, all adolescent inpatients were required to go to group therapy, but it soon became apparent that this created difficulties because of the haphazard composition of the group that resulted.

The problems arose in several areas. First, there were sometimes differences in the developmental levels of the adolescents who were referred. Adolescents of similar ages often differed greatly in maturity levels. Having group members who were developmentally in late adolescence with youngsters who were more preadolescent made it difficult for the group to form an identity or deal with common themes.

In addition, the developmentally older adolescents were often threatened by the behavior of the younger group members, the same behavior having been only recently and tentatively mastered on their part. The more advanced members would become impatient and angry with immature behavior that was "too close to home." They would often close down completely in the group, or they would scapegoat the less mature members. Depending on the group composition, it was at times counterproductive and at times potentially dangerous to those patients who were either psychotic or suffering from unusually high levels of anxiety to be added to the group. The very fragile patient might suffer more psychological damage by being in an anxiety-provoking group.

A reasonable group composition includes a balance of sameness and difference. We found that sameness was particularly important in terms of the developmental stage and the range of intellectual functioning. Less bright adolescents, without clearly developed abstract thinking skills, often felt lost and inadequate among the brighter group members and tended to act out or withdraw. Our group could accommodate adolescents who ranged from low average to bright normal. Major variations in either developmental or intellectual levels, however, tended to impede the group's progress and necessitated the formation of other groups.

Difference was important in terms of behaviors and diagnoses, and we tried to avoid having a group loaded with any particular type of diagnosis or behavior. Placing all depressive, psychotic, or acting-out adolescents in one group presented a host of problems, but a mixed group created an opportunity for learning, problem solving, and psychological growth.

The other problem that lack of screening presented was that, since we had no contact with members before they came to the initial group, we had no opportunity to engage them in the beginnings of a relationship, to orient them to the norms of the group, or to contract with them about their behavior in the group. Adolescents who were automatically referred come to the group ambivalent about being in therapy. They were brought to group therapy much as they were enrolled in school, with all the ambivalence and mixed feelings that implies. They did not see the group as a privilege, as we would have liked them to.

We also did not know what we were getting with each new member, and consequently could not predict or plan for the effect a member might have on the group. The lack of screening put us at a serious disadvantage as group therapists.

Anthony (1968), reflecting on his twenty-five years of work with groups, concluded that every therapist gets the group he deserves. This surely applied to our situation when we took referrals automatically without serious screening. Our first strategy was to request that the individual therapist who referred the patient to group therapy refer the patient to be screened first, knowing that some would not be placed in group immediately and some might be recommended for a different type of therapy. This approach took some selling to the staff, which was used to having all patients included in the same group. We also requested that patients be on the ward several weeks before being referred to group therapy screenings. We no longer wished to include adolescents who would be leaving the hospital after only a few sessions. With these changes in policy, we developed a formal screening process.

The screening interview became a valuable part of our overall group therapy program because it served a number of important functions. In addition to the obvious purpose of determining appropriateness or readiness for group, the screening interview was useful as a way of (1) building or enhancing the adolescent's motivation for group; (2) setting a clear contract for productive group work; (3) building a pregroup relationship; and (4) dealing with any significant ambivalence or resistance prior to entering group. In a sense, it became a type of preparation for group membership, or pregroup training.

During the screening interview, the co-therapists together talked with each adolescent. The patients were asked about previous group experiences; what they thought the group would be like (their preconceived assumptions); how the group might benefit them (their goals); how they could contribute to others in the group experience; about their ability to explore issues, disclose information, and give and receive feedback (ability to process, level of defensiveness); about any problems they anticipated so they could be dealt with; and whether they wanted to be in group (motivation). They were asked about their history and their reason for being hospitalized.

Through this process, an initial relationship was established. The therapists in turn explained what was expected of group members and described the types of issues that were frequently processed, such as family and sexual concerns. While these subjects were being discussed, the adolescents experienced a sample of the type of group discussion they might anticipate, and the therapists were able to gauge their responsiveness.

Adolescents who related well in the screening interview, felt comfortable talking about their history and problems, thought they would like to be in the group, and were prepared both to talk and listen to other members were accepted into the group and given a date for their first session. This acceptance essentially became a formal contract for being a group member. In many instances it was the first time our adolescent patients had negotiated successfully with adults about anything significant.

Another important aspect of the screening process, which had great impact on group functioning, was the way in which resistance was handled. Implicit in the screening interview was the clear message from the therapists that group membership was valuable and that it involved a clear set of expectations for doing productive work. It was made clear that group membership was not automatic or routine, and the therapists approached the screening interview almost as if the adolescent were applying for a position in the group.

Very often the adolescents showed initial resistance. Some had had prior group experiences that they saw as unproductive, uncomfortable, or boring. If the adolescents were motivated but uncertain about their ability to function in the group, the therapists would explore ways in which the group might help them deal with these obstacles. If they could make a commitment to try to overcome the obstacles, then group membership was considered a viable option.

It was clear from the outset that some patients were reluctant to make a contract to participate in group therapy. Usually the adolescents who had had bad group experiences viewed admission to group therapy as another hospital "requirement." If they were capable, but unmotivated or resistant to group, this was explored; however, the resistance had to be reasonably resolved and a commitment made before the adolescent was included in the group.

Often we would initially suggest or agree with the resistant adolescents that they were not ready for group, but that we would be willing to rescreen them later. We would sometimes ask the adolescents to suggest how long we should wait before another screening, or suggest that they might initiate it by contacting us when they felt ready, thereby placing more control in their hands.

Ambivalence is characteristic of many midadolescents, and our inpatients were no exception. We often received responses of ''maybe'' or ''I don't know'' or ''I might try but I don't know if I will talk in group.''

The ambivalent patient was the one who offered the most interesting challenge in the screening procedure and was also the one who benefited most from the following approach. When we encountered ambivalence, we would frequently split the patient's ambivalence by carrying on a dialogue in which one co-therapist took the ''pro'' position about becoming a group member and the other took the ''con'' position. One therapist might say, ''I can hear clearly that you're interested in group and are wanting to be with the other kids.'' The other might comment, ''Wait a minute, I hear him saying that it's not safe being a group member.'' This type of dialogue might go on for some time. The patient, in observing the dialogue, would often enter into the conversation, clarifying either the pro or the con stance with more information. Frequently, the ambivalence would be resolved and the patient would make a clear commitment to becoming involved in the group therapy. At other times, the screening ended with comments such as, ''Why don't we hold off making a contract to be in group therapy until you've had an opportunity to think about it and we will reinterview you at another time.''

The screening process was one way of beginning to engage the adolescent in a cooperative relationship. Although the therapists set the boundaries and offered assistance with obstacles, the ultimate responsibility for the adolescent's behavior (and consequently the decision on group membership) rested mainly with the adolescent, decreasing control issues associated with the group.

Theoretically, the screening process could be repeated until a mutual and satisfactory commitment was made. In reality, one screening interview was usually sufficient; and it was never necessary to hold more than two interviews in order to get a commitment.

Although occasionally there are adolescents who do not benefit from group therapy and may not be appropriate for a specific type of group, this particular aspect of the screening process was primarily designed to address resistance. Through the screening process, resistance could largely be resolved in order to prevent the adolescent from bringing it into the group setting. The resolution of the resistance, the engagement of the adolescent, the development of a contract, and the orientation of the adolescent as to what was expected in group all contributed to more productive group membership.

The process also contributed to increasing the prestige and value the adolescents attached to group therapy and enhancing their motivation for membership. This screening process eventually set the stage for the development of higher levels of group functioning.

SUMMARY

In reviewing varieties of adolescent group therapy, it becomes apparent that some adolescent group programs are oriented to specific issues: Some are designed to include adolescent volunteers; others focus on sexual issues, for sexual victims or offenders, or single-sex groups. In a broader context, some adolescent groups develop in the milieu, such as the "ward group" and the "Hub Group."

Our initial approach to developing an adolescent group therapy program was more open-ended and exploratory and was not oriented to one theme or problem. We simply tried to deal with all the adolescents on our unit but found this approach unrealistic. The difficulty in taking all referrals led us to develop a detailed screening interview to identify adolescents who were ready to participate in group therapy. The screening process enhanced the prestige of our group on the unit and set the stage for higher levels of group functioning.

4

PHYSICAL SETTINGS

> A mind is not to be changed by place or time, the mind is its own place, and in itself can make a Heaven of Hell, or Hell of Heaven.
>
> —John Milton

This chapter focuses on several important aspects of the physical setting for adolescent group therapy. Initially, we examine various systems of interpersonal communication. Then we discuss proxemics, non-verbal communication, and paralinguistics. Lastly, we reflect on the impact of the physical environment on our group's development.

SYSTEMS OF INTERPERSONAL COMMUNICATION

Several theories provide a basis for our understanding of the impact of the physical setting on patterns of communication. Most significant for our purposes are the theories of Patterson (1987) and Argyle and Dean (1965).

Hall's (1966) system for studying nonverbal communication was described in his analysis of proxemic behavior. He took eight factors into account: posture, orientation (physical positioning), functional distance, touch, visual behavior, thermal cues, olfactory cues, and voice loudness.

Other researchers (such as Argyle and Dean), in attempting to understand the management and expression of interpersonal communication and intimacy, examined behavioral changes occurring when interpersonal distance, gaze, smiling, and verbal intimacy interact. In a series of studies covering many years, consistent findings have emerged.

When interpersonal distance is decreased to the point of discomfort, eye contact decreases, smiling vanishes, and verbal intimacy decreases. Manipulation of each variable produced a comprehensive description relating to the variables explored, although in total they do not include all aspects of nonverbal communication.

Patterson's approach is more comprehensive, including proxemics and intimacy and the following: interpersonal distance, gaze, touch, body orientation, lean, facial expressiveness, duration of talking, interruptions, postural openness, relational gestures, nodding, and paralinguistics. Patterson describes the purposeful or functional utility of his system and the role of each factor in providing information, regulating interaction, expressing intimacy, exercising social control, and facilitating service or task goals.

We include systems for examining the human aspect of the physical setting in order to point out important areas in the behavior of group members. Most of these behaviors had their origins in infancy and childhood, and they may provide clues to deeper issues within the individual, who may be unwilling or unable to verbally communicate them. We would not attempt to interpret specific behaviors, since the uniqueness and individuality of many behaviors make such an interpretation virtually impossible. But the therapist receives behavioral signals that may be followed and explored.

PROXEMICS

With the publication of his work on nonverbal communication dealing with the shape of our interpersonal space, Hall provided a basis for an awareness of how the distances between people determine, in part, the degree of intimacy of the interpersonal communication. Thus, the greater the distance, the more superficial the communication.

The problem, however, is much more complex, and includes postural-sex identifiers: sociofugal-sociopetal orientation, ranging from face-to-face to a side-by-side positioning; kinesthetic factors dealing with the closeness of two people, ranging from touching to being able to touch only with reaching; the amount of touching between people; visual accessiblity; thermal factors, or the detection of body heat; loudness of communication; and smell.

The first five factors will influence group behavior and produce both approach and avoidance responses in others by how members present themselves. Body heat and smell have a minimal impact in most settings, although smell can have a major impact on a group if a member does not bathe, uses excessive perfume, or in other ways does not conform to cultural norms.

All these factors, which play a role in the communication process, are influenced by the therapists' arrangement of the physical space, including lighting, ventilation, and placement of chairs. Patients often alter the physical space, moving closer to someone with whom they wish to interact, as during the "pairing phase" described by Bion (1961), or by turning their chairs, pulling back, or other actions that modify the physical space.

While we are conscious of these factors and note carefully variations in the physical environment, they tend to have less impact than do factors relating to distances, which speak to the quality of communication.

Hall's data do not include seated distances, but it would seem that a group member should be no more than twelve feet from the opposite person and that a circular seating arrangement would be best, with the distance between chairs no more than two and a half feet. The size of the group, based on opportunities for communication, should be no more than seven persons, although with extended time periods of one and a half to two hours or two or more sessions per week, as many as ten members could be included. Two therapists bring the total to between nine and twelve people, which will fill most rooms set aside for group therapy. Thus a small room of sixteen by sixteen feet would allow for reduced social distances and create an atmosphere for intimate communication. This is not to say that communication will necessarily occur, but the climate approximates that in which it normally does.

Chairs should be similar and not assigned, although group members tend to identify certain seats as theirs or as the therapists'. No research exists that evaluates this factor. One's own personal style is undoubtedly the most important factor in the selection of seating. Control and closeness to the therapists may be a source of conflict among group members who vie to be in a position nearest, or sometimes farthest, from the therapists.

Therapists should be seated in positions that allow them to maintain a high level of visual contact with everyone in the room, including each other. Thus, anywhere on an angle of 135° or greater from each other is suggested.

NONVERBAL COMMUNICATION

Statements by Mehrabian (1971) suggest that in judging the validity of verbal statements, the speaker's facial expression carries more weight than what is said. For effective therapy, we must have clear visual access to all group members. This extends beyond facial expression and includes all other nonverbals, such as posture and gestures.

For easier understanding, gestures and expressive movements have been placed in five categories. Adolescents' nonverbals do not appear to be significantly different from adults' nonverbals. They are learned, largely by imitation, from earliest childhood. Occasional fads and group signals are developed but do not play a major role in nonverbal communication other than as identifying entry signals or for special situations. (In one group, "high fives" were given by all males in the group to each other for successful experiences.) For our purposes, the most significant nonverbal behaviors are those that accompany verbal communication, are used in lieu of verbal messages, or directly express an emotion.

Additionally, we would encourage an awareness of the therapists' nonverbals. Few experienced therapists have failed to encounter observations by patients about the therapist's mood, concerns, health, agitation, and other issues that had been reflected in nonverbal displays. Glancing at a clock or a watch or failing to make eye contact may be unconscious attempts by a therapist to regulate or limit interactions with clients, or to avoid certain uncomfortable issues.

The five nonverbals of special concern are:

> Illustrators: nonverbal behaviors that accompany verbal messages and demonstrate the message content. For instance, when instructing someone on how to drive a car, we typically engage in nonverbal acts such as pushing in the clutch and applying brakes.
>
> Affect displays: facial and body movements that express emotional meaning such as anger, fear, happiness, or sadness. These are not fully controlled behaviors and often reveal to others our true feelings and opinions despite protests to the contrary. Of the nonverbals, affect displays are the least subtle and the most significant. Therapists, too, emit affect displays, and their appearance may require processing either with the group or with the cotherapist.
>
> Regulators: nonverbal behaviors that operate to regulate or control the communications of others. Leaning toward another or using the Rogerian positive head nod are prime examples of regulators used to encourage additional communication.
>
> Adaptors: nonverbals that serve a particular need such as scratching an itch or picking one's nose. Adaptors tend to be less fully expressed in public, though one of the authors had a group member who constantly used adaptors to shock other group members and draw attention to himself. Some adaptors have dynamic significance and may reflect an unexpected emotion. For example, one group member constantly cleared his throat and had trouble swallowing. The difficulty related to his inability to swallow his rage toward his father.
>
> Emblems: nonverbals used in place of words or phrases. They

typically communicate a clear message, as signaling for someone to sit by you or accompany you, raising a hand to signal "stop," or holding one's nose in response to a comment.

It is important to be aware of and examine the nonverbals of group members. Too often we become immersed in words and lose the richness of nonverbals. In supervision of therapists in training, audiotaping provides the verbal behaviors and paralinguistics but loses the nonverbals of both therapists and clients.

PARALINGUISTICS

On the most concrete level, both esthetics and colors communicate a great deal to both therapists and clients. Furnishings may enhance or inhibit communication and the comfort of participants. So significant is this in the design of space that a national organization of architects and psychologists, Environmental Design Research Association, has emerged to speak to and research these issues.

A study was conducted many years ago by Maslow and Mintz (1956) in an attempt to determine whether individual judgments were affected by the room settings in which they were made. They used three rooms defined as beautiful, average, and ugly. The beautiful room contained paintings, carpeting, and comfortable seating. The average room resembled a typical faculty office. The ugly room was painted gray and was lighted by an overhead bulb. It was dirty, the ashtrays were full, and the room was in poor condition. Judgments made in the beautiful surroundings were judged as having more energy and well-being, while those made in less favorable surroundings were judged much less favorably, showing fatigue and displeasure. In a follow-up study, Mintz (1956) extended the work and found that judgments made in the ugly room over time were quicker (avoidance) and continued to be highly negative.

The implication from other works, particularly as it applies to reducing the hospital appearance of inpatient therapy settings, cannot be minimized. If therapy settings can provide comfort at the outset, then factors related to comfort can be eliminated or reduced as part of the business that occurs in therapy.

THE PHYSICAL ENVIRONMENT

Recent research, primarily from environmental and communications researchers, underscores the importance of the arrangement of physical space for the verbal and nonverbal communications of persons in groups. Seemingly minor factors such as a perceived hierarchy in the desirability of available seating, accessibility to possible viewers, the interposition of physical barriers like large tables, and the fixed positioning of chairs can become significant factors.

A spacious room in which chairs are widely spaced can reduce the level of intimacy in communication (Argle and Dean, 1965), while chairs too closely grouped create for many, at least in the American culture, a feeling of spatial invasion that reduces communication, limits eye contact, and results in great discomfort for the person who has been "invaded."

There are additional factors in this complex equation, such as where the co-therapists sit in relation to group members and each other. Therapists seated beside one another can create a "power corner," which can give participants a feeling of appearing before a parental tribunal. As a result, therapists tend to approach a 180° separation from each other. This allows maximum observation of group members, while permitting full communication between therapists, both verbal and nonverbal.

Wolfe (1975), in an important early attempt to deal with the physical settings in group psychotherapy, focused on the hospital ward environment and its appropriate usage and influence on groups. There was no clear data base in their research and their major arguments were supported by opinion rather than research.

Most important in our consideration is that the area in which group psychotherapy is conducted is part of a larger social system. It is embedded in and inextricably related to whatever system it is serving, whether in a hospital, a prison, or an outpatient facility. At some point, the group will look at how this room relates to the mission of the center. Even more salient is the potential for intrusion into the group by that system by means real or imagined, such as one-way mirrors, sound systems, rules (such as bans on smoking), room maintenance, and the types of seating available.

OUR EXPERIENCE

As we have seen from the research, the physical setting of the group has an important and often underestimated impact on the group's development. The attractiveness of the room, the amount of space, seating arrangement, privacy, and flexibility of the space are all factors that must be considered.

We decided to meet for our group therapy in a moderately large and comfortable room in the outpatient clinic, which was next door to the adolescent inpatient unit. Going "next door" to the outpatient clinic for group therapy was viewed positively by the adolescents and helped separate the group therapy from the politics and the occasional chaos that might be occurring in the unit. It also seemed to imply a greater sense of privacy, as the adolescents "went off" to group, much as adolescents might leave their own homes to go to an outpatient therapy program. As our group evolved, it took on more of a feel of an outpatient group, as do most ward groups, even though all the members lived together in the same ward.

The room was furnished with comfortable couches and chairs that could accommodate approximately eight adolescents and two co-therapists. This room was also used as a multipurpose room for intake screenings and family therapy and had two microphones and two large one-way mirrors for observation. Unfortunately, this was the room in which the adolescents had been screened prior to admission to the adolescent unit, and thus it was often associated with painful memories. Although the group had to work through the presence of the mirrors and microphones, in the long run the observation capabilities of the room offered us tremendous flexibility in our choice of group structure and our ability to provide training.

One response to the physical setting consisted of discussions about who might be behind the mirror. The therapists were always open about who was viewing, why they were there, and the promise of confidentiality. Members were always told when observers were present. If there was noise in the observation room when no observers were known to be present, the group stopped and sought an explanation by delegating a member to check the room. To further reduce the mystery, members were permitted to inspect the room, look through the mirror, and examine the sound system.

In one particularly poignant experience, an adolescent who was acting out and who had a strong feeling of rejection was deeply touched at learning that her therapist was watching the group. She seemed shocked that the therapist had that level of caring and concern for her. The mirror also elicited clowning, preening, and even surprised responses by the therapists when taking note of their reflections.

In general, the one-way mirrors caused little distraction over the life of the group and offered a view of reactions and behaviors that might have gone unnoticed in a different environment.

Differences in the types of available seating can present special problems. Couches offered several problems, especially for adolescents. First, they were highly favored by group members, who would race to secure them, refuse to share them, and frequently used them to absent themselves from the discussion. In some instances they fell asleep; in other cases they used the couch as a barrier. One severely disturbed female used the couch in a sexually explicit manner, which was unnerving to some of the male group members and produced anger in the female participants. While the situation was handled quickly and effectively, uniform seating without couches has worked best.

SUMMARY

This chapter presented important dimensions for the therapist to consider in providing an optimum environment for group psychotherapy. Factors related to appropriate interpersonal distance, freedom from distracting environmental elements, seating, decor, and positioning of the co-therapists were described. While it is possible to conduct effective group therapy under difficult environmental conditions, the energy and distractibility of most adolescent participants suggest that an optimal climate should be established.

5

TECHNIQUES, START-UP, AND DEVELOPMENT

> There is always one moment in childhood when the door opens and lets the future in.
>
> —Graham Greene
> *The Power and the Glory*

Questions on how to start and then maintain an adolescent group therapy program are powerful issues for the novice as well as the seasoned adolescent group therapist. Initially, this chapter will review some of the techniques that have been developed for working with groups. Secondly, the chapter presents a chronological review of our adolescent group, with emphasis on techniques and tactics that evolved.

VIDEOTAPE

Adolescent group therapists have reported using videotape to deal with various problems. Mavrit, Lind, and McLaughlin (1974), working with antisocial adolescents, divided the youngsters into videotaped groups and nonvideotaped groups. The videotaping was seen as increasing the reality-based self-other concept and reflection. An additional benefit for the videotaped group members was a decreased need for activity in order to cope.

Weber (1980) did a controlled study examining the effects of videotape playback on adolescents' expressions of warmth and hostility and on flight. The first half of the session was videotaped, resulting in an increase in expressions of warmth and a decrease in flight; hostility, however, remained about the same. An additional gain for the group was that its cohesiveness seemed to improve with the use of videotape.

NONVERBAL TECHNIQUES

Olsson and Myers (1972) saw nonverbal techniques, including role-playing and sensitivity-training methods, as very useful tools in an adolescent group. His group consisted of six to eight patients, ages fourteen to sixteen, with two male co-therapists. A recurring theme in the group was drugs. The group leaders used a technique of "laying on of hands" to help one group member "think straighter in group," and a touching exercise to reassure a female member of her physical attractiveness. Other exercises included building group cohesiveness and working with a youngster who was isolating himself from the group.

The therapists felt that nonverbal techniques in adolescent groups need to be handled authoritatively with careful limit setting by the therapists. They felt this approach demands innovation on the part of the therapist and encourages creative perceptiveness in group members. Finally, they saw the use of nonverbal techniques as a helpful method of raising and dealing with adolescent dilemmas.

POETRY AND THERAPEUTIC GAMES

Mazza (1981) argues strongly for the use of poetry as a therapeutic tool in treating the troubled adolescent. He cautions that the technique, like any other intervention, requires fine-tuned judgment around timing and purpose. The technique itself can be varied from sharing a poem with a client to encouraging clients to write poetry to developing collaborative poems in a group or family context.

According to Mazza, the collaborative poem, in which each member contributes a line, can be useful in adolescent groups. Often, a poem by an established poet or a popular song can be helpful in stimulating the group process. Mazza warns, however, that if the technique is perceived as too academic or intellectual, it will be rejected by some adolescents, and among very bright adolescents it may reinforce the defense mechanism of intellectualization.

Bernet (1982) developed a technique that bridges the gap between the early adolescent's need to be very active in group and the lack of maturity needed to deal with problems in an exclusively verbal mode. He based his technique on the "Talking, Feeling, Doing Game" developed by Gardner (1975). The patients, ages twelve to fourteen, were in treatment at the Children's Unit of the Psychiatric Institute, a private psychiatric hospital in Washington, D.C. The group meeting consisted of about eight patients and two co-therapists. A ritual of introducing and orienting new members and electing a president and sergeant-at-arms began each group. The co-therapists' chief function was to maintain a constant balance between order and spontaneity. The content of the group included a detective game, a sex question game, and jokes and riddles.

Bernet felt that his verbal game technique meets the needs of the early adolescent and is essentially a transition technique between the activity therapy used with children and the purely verbal therapy used with older adolescents.

Corder, Whiteside, and Vogel (1977) developed another therapeutic game, based on a game Corder had used in earlier work with adolescents (1975). The game had an item pool with the categories Knowing Yourself, Understanding Each Other, and Problem Solving. The items in each category were classified into five levels of difficulty: neutral warm-up item, mildly difficult social problems, positive self-disclosures, negative self-disclosures, and deepest self-revelation. The group members rolled dice and moved their game pieces to squares on the game board. Each player had a "pass" card for items that were too difficult. The author indicated that the game materials were developed as an adjunct to group therapy sessions with adolescents ages thirteen to eighteen with IQs of 80 and above.

Other therapists who use therapeutic game materials report that they are highly useful and flexible tools that lend themselves to many different stages of adolescent group therapy.

BEHAVIORAL TECHNIQUES

A behavioral technique used by Rosenstock and McLaughlin (1982) called "positive group" requires adolescents to make positive statements about themselves and other group members. Each adolescent must then acknowledge the compliment paid him or her. Proscribed are all negative comments. The positive group experience was found to be facilitative over a broad range of diagnostic categories and helped enhance group members' self-images, social skills, and leadership potential. Positive group is recommended for inpatients as well as outpatient adolescent groups.

Other behavioral techniques have been used to help stabilize generalized acting out in adolescent groups and to control anger and facilitate affective empathy. Bardill (1977) has done extensive work in behavioral contracting with preadolescent and adolescent groups. His population included males from nine to fourteen years of age. The essence of his behavior contracting approach was the agreement of "something for something" between the therapist and the group members. The contracting arrangement called for each boy to earn points for specific behaviors during the therapy session. At the end of a month the points were converted into money, at the rate of a penny per point. Therapeutic responses by group members were defined as listening to others, making comments designed to be helpful to others, either supportive or confrontational, and talking about personal concerns.

This technique, according to its originator, enabled the group therapists to shift their attention from control issues to those of enhancing the therapy process. Essentially, therapists using the techniques reported that their sessions were characterized by a meaningful therapeutic atmosphere. When destructive reactions occurred, other group members seldom got caught up in the disruptive behavior.

Fiendler et al. (1986) used cognitive-behavioral techniques for the self-control of anger and aggressive behavior in institutionalized male adolescents. Compared to a waiting-list control group and a control group within the ward, the cognitive-behavioral patients increased their reflectiveness and their self-control. Interestingly, as the group began to gain control of anger in the group meetings, this control then generalized to the ward, with a subsequent decrease in fines and restrictions.

Kaplan and Phillips (1981) compared ten male and ten female nondelinquents on a structured, self-reported, affective empathy task; an unstructured, affective empathy task; and a cognitive role-taking measure. Differences between groups were found only on the unstructured empathy task, with delinquents performing more poorly than nondelinquents. Within the delinquent sample, males demonstrated less empathy than females on the structured empathy task.

SILENT OBSERVERS

In a short-term, inpatient psychiatric unit, Oldham (1982) developed a specialized group therapy approach. In conjunction with initiating a modified therapeutic-community model in his unit, the group therapy program was changed from a traditional format—two co-therapists, selected patients meeting twice a week, and the group playing a peripheral role in the unit—to having all unit staff members present for all group meetings as silent observers. Benefits reported from this innovative approach were that communication concerning the patients became more effective, the group therapy became centrally important to the unit staff and patients, and there was a minimization of the transference, rivalries, and distortion often seen in longer-term groups or in groups lacking structure or objective tasks.

EARLY PROBLEMS

Our adolescent group met twice a week for one hour, from three to four, usually on Tuesday and Thursday afternoons. The patients left school at 2:30 P.M., walked to the adolescent unit, often had a snack, and them came to group therapy. We soon discovered that snacking after school was very important to our adolescents, and initially some of them brought food to the group. This served both positive and negative functions, depending on the stage of group development and how the group was functioning. We also observed that midafternoon is a high energy time for some adolescents and a time of fatigue for others.

Each new patient in the unit was assigned a clinical counselor as a case manager-advocate. These clinical counselors were responsible for seeing that their patients were attending treatment activities and for raising issues at staff meetings if their patients were not getting the proper treatment. The clinical counselors presented themselves at the group therapy sessions with their respective patients and remained for the initial session.

This turned out to be a very awkward situation, and a clear cue to the patients that we, as a staff, were not communicating well with each other. The situation continued for a few sessions until we had a series of meetings with the clinical counselors. We finally discovered that the clinical counselors, who at this point were not meeting as frequently as they had been prior to the opening of the unit, were feeling a loss of group support and wanted to recapture that group experience by coming to the adolescent group.

After processing this issue with the group members, a consensus was reached that certain clinical counselors and staff from the unit could observe the group, providing the members knew ahead of time which days they were to be observed and who would be doing the observing. The agreement proved to be a disaster in one sense, but dramatically raised the issues of privacy and confidentiality in the group therapy program.

The disaster occurred when a clinical counselor confronted an adolescent in the unit with data gained from his observation of the group. This break of confidentiality set in motion a series of group sessions focusing on privacy. The group members, in their own words, reminded us of the many times their privacy had been violated in family situations, foster care, and other institutions. The issue of privacy led to discussions about the treatment philosophy of the unit regarding respect, trust, and confidentiality. The patients perceived that certain clinical counselors were too involved in their behavior, which they saw as essentially controlling and disrespectful rather than caring and concerned.

Listening to the complaints about some of the clinical counselors, we experienced a dilemma faced time and time again by group therapists in adolescent units and to some degree by group therapists in other settings. Under the stress of hospitalization, adolescents often organize their world into "good guys" and "bad guys" and their treatment interventions into "good" and "bad." So when we agreed to talk about the "bad guys," to some degree we fragmented the treatment programs.

But if we had chosen not to address their concerns, we would have left the members with the impression that certain important aspects in their overall treatment could not be processed in group.

We asked the group members how they intended to deal with the clinical counselors they thought were being too intrusive. We tried to support the idea that the issue was a problem that needed to be solved, rather than giving the impression that some of the clinical counselors fell into the category of "bad guys." One adolescent responded, "I'll just tell the bastard to back off." Another patient confronted us with, "What the hell are you going to do about stuff going out of the group?" This theme continued until we worked out a procedure in which the patients brought up their concerns at a unit meeting, and we discouraged the staff from observing the group. It is our impression that these maneuvers lowered the status of the group therapy program in the unit, because we were perceived as siding with the patients, being defensive about observation, and not caring about the overall adolescent treatment program. Following the decision against observation, however, there was a marked improvement in the functioning of the group, with fewer negative feelings.

Our fantasy was that we were simply working through some start-up problems and that things would get better from this point on. That was a serious mistake. We had not been experiencing the start-up pains of an adolescent group; we were simply having a discussion group about how the adolescent unit was functioning.

Several more patients were admitted to the unit and placed in group therapy, again after a very superficial get-acquainted type of screening. The group now numbered six members, and it seemed that our therapy program was under way. The members, four males and two females, seemed to deal with the ambiguities and anxieties of the group situation by pairing up and sharing information about where they came from and their prior hospitalization, and trying to discover mutual acquaintances.

These dyads were hard for us to penetrate, and there appeared to be few group dynamics evolving. When a theme did develop, it was generally about some environmental issue such as a teacher, a nurse, or a clinical counselor the patients disliked. Sometimes they would gossip about a new patient on the unit in terms of how "weird" or "crazy" he appeared.

Our attempts to facilitate the development of themes for the whole group to work on or to interpret their anger toward an authority figure were ignored or generated responses such as, "Are you kidding?" or "That doesn't make sense!" or "There you go again!" There was very little direct confrontation by the adolescents with the co-therapists. Rather, they tended to ignore our input. The group atmosphere was characterized by a sense that it was safe only to be involved superficially with each other, to complain about environmental events or people outside the group, and to distrust the co-therapists.

We continued to be active in the group, but at times passively endured the lack of productivity and had trouble waiting for a more productive phase of the group. In retrospect, we know that the adolescents sensed our anxiety about how poorly the group was functioning.

The difficult period did not last very long because some patients ran away from the unit and were hospitalized in a more secure unit. Other patients were taken out of the unit by their parents because of conflicts with the staff over treatment philosophy. As with all groups in which membership decreases suddenly, there was a painful regression. The unit was undergoing its own upheaval, with some staff leaving and new staff, who had not gone through the exciting and meaningful start-up phase of the unit, coming in. This tightening-up phase saw much more confrontation by the patients, more use of restriction, and less processing of issues.

The regression of the group for the five remaining patients took the form of early resistances such as withdrawal, with members simply not talking, going to sleep, getting up and walking around the room, or playing with the furniture, particularly the microphones. The patients would accuse each other of saying negative things outside the group. On occasion they questioned the co-therapists, asking, "Why the hell do we have group therapy?"

There was so much disruptive individual and group behavior going on that it was very hard to work on anything or prioritize issues. This stage of therapy was chaotic, fragmented, and disorganized, and was characterized by negative leadership by group members and the testing of the co-therapists' resolve to continue the group therapy program. These negative behaviors began to turn us into wardens. We were setting limits, asking the adolescents not to do certain things, and trying to ignore some of the negative input. There seemed to be a collective effort on their part to see what our endurance level was for their acting out. The situation also seemed to be a test of whether we would put them on restriction and stop the group for a while. They apparently wanted to see if we would deal with them as the unit staff was dealing with them.

CO-THERAPIST SUPPORT

At times we were very frustrated and overwhelmed by the way the group was operating. If we had been doing the group alone, we probably would have quit, but we discussed our negative feelings about the adolescents and realized that we needed to establish a therapeutic presence in the group.

In examining our style, we found that our verbal and nonverbal input was very restricted. In a sense, the adolescents were shaping our behavior just as they had shaped some of the unit staff's and their individual therapists' behavior. We were not playing the variety of roles MacLennan and Felsenfeld (1968) say are needed in order for group members to develop self-responsibility: teacher, reflector, informant, resource person, explorer, model for identification, clarifier, interpreter, transmitter of values, and support person. Once we acknowledged our painful situation, we began to examine the specific problems confronting us and the strategies we could develop to address them meaningfully.

One problem we became aware of was that in initial sessions we usually sat near each other or on the same side of the room. That kept us at a distance from the adolescents and created a we-they kind of arrangement. In a sense it actually kept us out of the group. We began to sit opposite each other, which enabled us to maintain eye contact, communicate nonverbally, "spread our weight" around the room, and "gain territory" in the group.

The adolescents immediately commented on the change, saying things like, "What are you guys up to?" or "I think you're trying to divide us up," or "I want you to sit over there." We gave them some nonverbal approval for their observations but remained seated across from one another. We felt that this very simple change might have benefits in future sessions.

Another problem was that the adolescents often developed "resistant alliances," in which two members would sit together and consistently act out. We began to ask them to change places with other members or with one of the therapists, explaining that we needed to "spread the energy around the room."

Adolescents who were acting out tended to congregate on the two couches in the room. We put the couches opposite one another and each of us began to take over one of the couches. This, of course, required us to get to the room before the adolescents did.

Another way we used the seating arrangement was by having a cotherapist sit beside an acting-out adolescent in order to help control the adolescent's behavior through physical proximity, or to sit by a "weak" member in order to add power to that member's position. As we experimented with our positions in the group, we gained an appreciation of the importance of our physical presence and used it in different ways at different stages in the group process for a variety of therapeutic purposes.

SETTING THE TONE

Another observation we made was that at the beginning of each group we had been waiting patiently for material to be generated by group members. Sometimes we would have a few moments of silence broken by an episode of acting out, followed by laughter, and then more of the same. So we developed specific tactics for beginning the sessions.

If one group member was present in the room before the group started, we would immediately engage the member in a discussion about how the day was going and give him or her some emotional support. This allowed us to develop an alliance with one member and, more important, set the tone for the upcoming group. As the rest of the group members arrived, they found a dialogue already in process, which made a shift into a full group discussion easier.

If some of the group members arrived and were behaving disruptively, we could ignore them because of the "mini" group session with the member who had come early. If the disruptive behavior was too much to ignore, we could say, "Excuse us, we are trying to listen to what Joe is telling us." This tactic helped, but in no way did it completely solve the discordant behavior in the group.

An interesting thing we discovered was that some group members were trying to cooperate and actually reinforced our approach by coming early to group and participating in the mini group. The uncooperative members of the group were often critical and rejecting of those members.

A variation of this strategy was our attempt to disarm the resistance. Often there was one adolescent who consistently acted out or was a negative group leader. We would create a way to compliment him or her before he or she had the opportunity to act out in the group or to influence others to do so. We had to respond quickly. We would find a way to compliment the particular adolescent on arrival, often as he or she crossed the threshold of the group therapy room. Sometimes this was problematic or required creative thinking, as the member was often negative and difficult to compliment. Resorting to statements such as, "I like your T-shirt" (or tennis shoes or haircut), we would distract the adolescent from disruptive behavior and focus on cooperative exchanges. This tactic, in combination with the mini group, often helped us set the necessary therapeutic tone early in the group session.

RESISTANCE

Any therapeutic endeavor, whether on an individual basis or on a group level, will be met by resistance. Without dealing effectively with resistance, very little therapy can go on, and nowhere is this better understood than in working with adolescents in group therapy.

Let us begin by thinking about the word *resistance* in its broadest sense as it applies to group therapy with adolescents. From a negative standpoint, resistance has the connotation of being noncurative. In a sense it prevents the group from developing into a safe context in which important issues can be dealt with meaningfully.

In our group, the resistant maneuvers were natural building blocks to be encountered in order for the group to be a richer and more meaningful experience later. The resistances such as complaining, silence, acting out, and scapegoating were old behaviors or survival techniques used previously by the adolescents to protect themselves in frightening or anxiety-provoking group situations.

These resistances, as Rosenthal (1971) pointed out, may be viewed as performing vital functions. They indirectly convey the members' respective life histories to the co-therapists and provide excellent hints about the kinds of emotional difficulties each member has experienced. The resistances also enable group members to adjust to the emotional stress created by group membership and the array of feelings and impulses aroused within the dynamic matrix of group therapy.

Understanding the resistances, their origins and meaning, and the feelings they were designed to contain greatly enhanced our understanding of the group and its members. As we studied the emerging group and individivual resistances, understood the emotional experiences that produced them, and led the group members to a gradual understanding of them, we energized and supported the group members' maturational strivings and furthered our own emotional and professional growth.

TESTING THE CO-THERAPIST: COMPLAINING

Our group members continued to complain about privacy and confidentiality. They were very concerned about what the co-therapists shared with the treatment teams and what we wrote in their charts. The group members were testing us on how much we could be trusted with information from the group sessions. Also, they were asking us how closely we were aligned with the other staff and the rules of the unit, and how closely we were aligned with them. Another concern was what we would do about information that came up in group involving a member who might actually or potentially be harmful to himself or someone else.

The group members wanted to know implicitly whether we would panic and run to the staff about every infraction of the rules discussed in group, or whether we would collude with serious acting out by group members and do nothing. These questions could only be answered by dealing with the material as it presented itself in subsequent sessions.

We confronted the issue of reporting to the treatment team by explaining that we kept the treatment members informed about the general progress of the group. For example, we told the group members that we might say to the treatment team, "The group is still in the phase of building trust and seems to be making adequate progress." We gave them an example of a recent note on a chart, which stated, "Today in group therapy we discussed issues about privacy and confidentiality. This issue is very important to all members and will require more discussion in subsequent groups." Giving concrete examples of what we told the treatment team and wrote in their medical records seemed to reassure the group members that we could be trusted in these areas. Some of the adolescents needed to know exactly what we put in their medical records, and they managed to get access to their records from some of the clinical counselors, particularly those on the night shift to check our notes and other data.

As we looked back on this issue of reporting on the group, it became evident that this was the beginning of a series of tests of our capacity to deal with complicated issues in the group. As the privacy/confidentiality issue subsided on an overt level, one group member disclosed that he had smoked marijuana on his weekend pass. Joe had a history of drug abuse and had made a contract with his individual therapist that his weekend pass would be drug-free. After his disclosure, some group members supported his use of marijuana, saying that he could do whatever he wanted when he was at home. Other group members, particularly those who knew about his history of drug abuse, seemed to disapprove nonverbally, but did not actually condemn his smoking the marijuana.

We saw the marijuana issue as a great opportunity for the group to do some useful work together. Approaching Joe's disclosure with a great deal of curiosity, we avoided focusing on how it violated the unit rules and his contract with his individual therapist. Instead, we asked him how he had decided to smoke marijuana. He revealed that some of his friends had come by on Saturday night, and they all went out and smoked. We asked if he wanted to smoke and he admitted he did. Later, as we processed the issue, it became clearer that he had trouble turning down the opportunity to smoke because he wanted to be with his friends and out of his house for a few hours.

As the discussion continued, he seemed to become somewhat anxious about being the center of the group's attention. Instead of commenting on his anxiety, we supported the fact that he had brought up the issue by saying, "We're glad you had the courage to bring this up in group and that you thought the group was a safe enough place to talk about such an important thing."

One of the group members asked Joe in a very kind way if he had been worried prior to his pass about whether he would get involved with drugs. He responded, "No." Then we asked him if his parents were concerned about his becoming involved with drugs again, and he again said, "No."

At this point, the group members became involved in his dilemma over wanting to be with his peer group and possibly not wanting to be involved with drugs. They acknowledged how hard it is to turn down a joint when you have smoked a lot with a particular group of friends. We responded by agreeing that it is difficult to stop old behaviors when you are with old friends.

We felt the group was going to press us to come up with a solution to the problem of a group member smoking marijuana on pass and violating unit rules and his contract. Our adolescents, like others in midadolescence, have the capacity to persuade adults to take over their problems, and we felt such a maneuver was about to occur, but we avoided that and offered no solution. Rather, we kept exploring how Joe and the others saw the dilemma, emphasizing that it was his problem and the group's problem.

Toward the end of the session, one group member said, "You're going to have to tell your individual therapist that you smoked on pass." We asked the group member why, and she responded, "'Cause you're not supposed to go back on your word." The ensuing discussion of responsibility in relationships centered on strong feelings that clinical counselors and therapists want to control everything patients do and that they do not really understand teenagers' problems. This discussion continued until the end of the session, when we asked Joe how he saw the issue now and whether he had developed a plan to deal with it. He said he was more confused now than when he initially brought it up. A group member suggested that we continue the discussion in the next group. Joe did not appear to be very interested in that suggestion. One day after the group, he discussed the smoking issue with his individual therapist and clinical counselor but did not bring it up in subsequent groups.

The work on Joe's smoking of marijuana on pass seemed to consolidate our style of being supportive about bringing up important material, exploring it extensively, not expecting quick solutions, and respecting the capacity of our adolescents to be socially responsible.

As soon as we began to feel somewhat more comfortable as co-therapists in group, another, much more complex issue was raised, calling for a modification of our style. It was also a clear reminder that flexibility and consistent communication are crucial for therapists dealing with troubled adolescents.

In one group session there seemed to be an unusual level of anxiety. Immediately after the session started, one member, Susan, indicated that she had something to tell the group about another group member. We asked her if the other group member had given her permission to broach the subject in group. We were careful to support the notion that one group member was concerned about a problem facing another member, but also sensitive to the fact that the dilemma was not being raised by the person involved. We had learned in other group situations that if you do not give the person who has the problem every opportunity to introduce it, you are seen as being disrespectful.

We then asked Mary, who had the problem, if she wanted the matter brought up in group. The group's tension was displayed nonverbally: some members lit cigarettes, some became fidgety, and some seemed to be indicating by visible levels of anxiety and distress that there was a need to deal with something special and important.

Susan was becoming anxious and said, "I'm just going to tell you what's going on." We supported the notion that she was apprehensive and had a burdensome role, but we still insisted that she check with Mary. So she asked Mary, who was her roommate, if she could tell the group what they had talked about the night before.

Mary appeared very depressed but somewhat relieved that the issue was coming up in group. We asked her if she would like to discuss the problem herself, and she said, "No," she would rather have her roommate tell the group. Emphasizing that it must be a very serious problem, we all promised to listen carefully and try to help if we could.

Susan said that Mary had talked to her about committing suicide and had hidden a razor blade under the sink in their room. This issue was obviously not in the same category as the marijuana smoking. We praised Susan for being courageous and concerned enough to bring this matter before the group and began to process the issue. In order to focus the group on the member with the potential for suicide, we quickly turned our attention to Mary, recognizing how hard it must have been to share the painful feelings about wanting to hurt herself. As the session progressed, it became evident that some of the adolescents knew about Mary's suicidal tendency.

At first Mary seemed somewhat reluctant to discuss her feelings, but she did not give any clear signals either verbally or nonverbally that she wished us to stop trying to deal with her. Susan pleaded with her to talk about her feelings and told her how much she liked her. Other group members also encouraged her to talk, although several seemed immobilized by the topic.

Mary began to reveal that she felt sad all the time and felt she could do nothing right. She talked about how she had taken pills two times prior to her hospitalizations in an attempt to kill herself. Everyone in the group listened to her and appeared mindful of her problem. As she disclosed more details, she seemed to become energized and somewhat brighter. We commented that she seemed less depressed than when she first started talking.

We recognized that the data produced about her suicide potential had to be dealt with immediately following the session; there could be no postponing the issue until the next group meeting. Acknowledging that it took a great deal of courage on her part to discuss her difficulties, we nonetheless told Mary that she had to come up with a plan in the remaining time to deal with her situation. She said matter-of-factly that she was feeling better because she had talked about her situation and that she was not going to harm herself. We supported her statement that she had made a commitment not to harm herself, but pointed out that feelings about harming oneself subside for a while and then may reemerge suddenly. Some of the group members did not like hearing this and complained, "She'll be all right; look, she's over it, don't bug her anymore!"

We continued to emphasize the potential for a recurrence of the feelings about hurting herself and urged her to tell someone on the unit as soon as the session was over what we had talked about, including where she had hidden the razor blade or anything else she could use to hurt herself. At this point Mary burst into tears, and her crying seemed to be a great relief to her. We waited until she regained her composure and asked her if she was ready to tell the unit staff about the suicide plans. She indicated that she wanted both of us with her when she told the head nurse about her problem, so after group we walked her to the unit and stayed with her until she was placed on suicide watch.

The processing in group of the marijuana smoking and the suicide plan brought us to the realization that our adolescents valued being talked to directly, but with much care and support. They valued consistency in our dealings with them, and it appeared that our consistency would be tested time and again. They were certainly shaping our behavior at this point. We felt they approved of our attempt to engage them in examining their behavior, but they actively rejected us whenever we seemed to be moving into an intrusive or invading control posture. We began to sense a level of synchronization between us and the group that had not been present in previous group sessions.

In our discussions with each other after the group sessions, we began to realize our adolescents wanted to perceive us in a particular way. They were asking us to be trustworthy, particularly as they shared their vulnerabilities with us. As they sorted out their feelings, they wanted us to be patient and sensitive. There was an expectation and a hope that we would be genuine with them, because they had each had painful experiences with adults who had not been sincere. In short, they wanted us to be empathetic and honest with them in dealing with their problems.

WITHDRAWAL

As the group continued, we were confronted with other resistances. On more than one occasion, we had a member, Jim, withdraw from the group by going to sleep. This resistance presented us with an interesting dilemma. Should we simply confront Jim with statements like, "The group is not a place for sleeping; please stay awake and participate"? Or should we ignore him because the confrontation would result in a power struggle? Neither approach had been successful in the past.

As we discussed the problem in the regular meetings we held after each group session, we realized how annoyed we were with Jim. We talked about confronting him directly and agreed that this would certainly produce a power struggle with him and, to some degree, cause a regression in the group's development. Again, we considered that perhaps we should just wait it out and eventually he would start to participate. But in a sense, we were doing just that and it wasn't solving the problem. By not dealing with Jim, we were colluding with his behavior, saying by our own inaction that sleeping in group therapy sessions was all right. Since we did not want to reinforce behavior that was not in the best interest of an individual member or the group as a whole, we decided that the most honest approach to this problem was to bring the matter up with the group the next time Jim went to sleep during a session, presenting it as the very real dilemma it was.

DILEMMA DISCLOSURE TACTICS

In the three group sessions that followed, Jim did not go to sleep, so we thought that this particular resistance had disappeared. The next session focused on friendship, particularly loyalty in relationships, and shortly into the session Jim began to doze off. Halfway through the session he appeared to be sound asleep.

Since the group theme was caring and loyalty in friendships, it seemed appropriate to demonstrate concern about Jim. The dilemma was presented by a co-therapist saying, "I'd like to bring up a tough problem to the group." The members seemed shocked that one of the co-therapists had a problem to bring up. One member commented, "Doc, I think you have more than one problem. Go ahead and tell us what's going on," which was followed by laughter.

The co-therapist continued, "I've got a dilemma about Jim's sleeping in group." Another group member said, sounding annoyed, "What are you bringing that up for?" The co-therapist responded, "Please, hear me out on this," and proceeded to say, "Listen, one part of me says that Jim has a right to do what he needs to do in group, including going to sleep, and another part of me says that if I don't try to find out why he is sleepy, I really don't care about him."

By now Jim's eyes were open and he appeared to be attentive to what was going on. The other co-therapist asked what the group thought about the dilemma. One group member said in a very supportive manner, "Every time Jim's medication is changed, he has problems staying awake. He even falls asleep in school."

We thanked the group member for the information about Jim's medication and revealed that we did not know about the problem. Then we asked Jim, "How long have you been having problems with your medication?" He answered, "Ever since I came in the hospital, the medicine has bothered me. I don't like taking it 'cause it makes me feel tired all the time."

Another group member said, "Why don't you leave him alone? Can't you see he doesn't want to talk in group?" The other co-therapist responded, "I'm not that clear that Jim doesn't want to participate in group."

Jim explained, "I have a hard time understanding some of the things talked about in group and sometimes I feel like I'd like to leave the group." The co-therapist expressed appreciation about knowing how difficult it was for Jim to be in the group.

Toward the end of this session, we asked Jim and the others to consider the possibility of discussing how we could make the group a place where Jim felt more like a full member. Jim and some of the group indicated they would like such a discussion in future groups. Caring about Jim and struggles over not feeling like a full member of the group was an important building block in the development of our group.

The dilemma-disclosure tactic began to be a regular method of dealing with certain individual resistances in the group. It was another way for us to be actively concerned, honest, and consistent with the group members. The tactic substantially cut down on the issue of colluding with individual resistances and consequently being inconsistent in dealing with negative behavior in the group. It allowed for active engagement of issues and a problem-oriented approach to caring. The tactic allowed for information about problems to be generated, decreased the possibility of power struggles, lessened defensiveness, and to a large extent prevented major regressions in the group process. The tactic became the basis for other, more sophisticated group interventions developed later.

SILENCE

Just as we began to feel a glimmer of success in the group, a new set of more powerful resistances surfaced. The first new resistance maneuver was that of silence. In our group, as in other groups, there are usually several reasons for silence. The most obvious was members' anger at us as group leaders, which was related to the possibility that we were making them too dependent on the group and getting too close to them psychologically. The adolescents did not feel safe, comfortable, or powerful enough to simply tell us how angry they were with us. Silence also made a nonverbal statement that they were not going to cooperate in a process that might prove to be dangerous or meaningless. It was a powerful tool for slowing down the group's development.

On a few occasions the episodes of silence were not generated by anger at us but were the product of some important issue going on within the adolescent culture of the unit. Usually the themes that induced silence concerned sex, drugs, leadership struggles among patients, or other typical adolescent issues. When these themes became intense outside the group, the members often became so intimidated that they elected to remain silent in group so they would not disclose the difficult theme operating in their culture.

Some therapists have talked about silence in groups as having a therapeutic or curative value, particularly when group meditation is a component. We often explored the possibility with our group that silence was being used in a reflective or meditative way, but we never experienced a time when silence was being used in a therapeutic or curative fashion.

In our discussions outside of group, we came to understand that silence was a resistance that was a natural part of our group's development. Realizing that almost all youngsters in midadolescence to late adolescence use the silence maneuver to deal with parents, peers, and teachers at certain times helped make it less threatening to us when it surfaced. Our most conservative method at this point in dealing with silence was simply to wait it out and hope it would disappear spontaneously. We used this approach several times with success.

There were, however, problems with waiting out the silent times. Silence appeared to be gaining more and more power and was becoming the norm after a few sessions. If we simply kept going along with the silent sessions, we were in a sense agreeing with the group members that the issues underlying the silence were too powerful to be dealt with there.

We saw the episodes of silence as a test of our ability to read the nonverbals going on in the group. We began to notice this behavior if the group members were exhausted by some difficult issue outside of the group, if they were angry at us, or if there were problems within dyads or factions within the group. At times the nonverbals were so mixed that it was difficult to discern precisely what might be the basis for the silence.

As a rule, we tried to help individual members break the silence rather than break it ourselves, saying in effect that being quiet was no longer the way they wanted the group to operate. Some group members would give clues through eye contact that they were about to talk, and an approving nod from one of us often was sufficient to get verbalization established. Sometimes the initiation of verbal statements by one member would quickly bring replies from other members, or half the group would talk while the other half remained silent.

During one session, one or two members began to talk after a period of silence, with minimal support from us, and were attacked verbally by other group members. In this situation, we felt it was important to allow those who talked to deal with the members who were attacking them, because this was a positive rather than a negative leadership struggle among the adolescents.

As the conflict developed, we became involved at an appropriate moment in trying to sort out the basis of the conflict, expressing curiosity about the dissension and being careful not to side with either faction. We were interested in exploring the parameters of the discord in depth and held off suggesting a solution, even though at times one seemed very evident to us.

In another dispute, the group members being attacked were essentially the objects of displacement, because the attackers were really angry at the co-therapists. We gently moved the discussion along until one group member made the observation, "You're really pissed off at them [the co-therapists] but you're taking it out on them [the group initiators]." This interpretation by a fellow group member was much more significant in facilitating the process than if either of us had made it.

If the silence in the group appeared to result from members' sadness or exhaustion, then we found it important to reflect that picture in a statement such as, "I've got a sense that something has everyone down in the group today and I'm wondering if this is the right time to begin looking at what it is." This comment acknowledged that we did not know precisely what was causing the silence, but we were willing to engage the group in exploring the problem. Sometimes this was a useful and successful tactic; at other times it was received with silence or was rejected with comments like, "Bug off."

If the nonverbals suggested that the silence was powered by a conflict between two group members or two factions in the group, we would attempt to bring it to the surface with statements like, "My guess is that today's silence in group has to do with some people in here having trouble getting along with each other." We would follow that up with, "Also, my guess is that there are some feelings that if we start to talk about—like trouble getting along—things will get out of hand and it will not be safe in here." Sometimes this comment was greeted with a response such as, "You're way off today, because the problem is that five of us were just put on ward restriction." Now the issue powering the silence was out, and we could begin to deal with it on a verbal level. If the contention that surfaced regarding the silence happened to be a pseudoissue, this would soon be discovered and processed by the group.

When we made a mistake in guessing what was going on in the group, it simply made us more human. We would never suggest that co-therapists should make blunders on purpose, because this would be seen as dishonest and manipulative by the group members and would be asking for martyrdom on the part of the co-therapists.

Accurate observations about individuals or factions within the group being at odds were usually followed by more silence. Then we would wait for more time to elapse, while the tension and anxiety would build. At this point we would say, "Rather than talk about the problem, why not explore the reasons not to talk about the problem." As simple as this approach seems, it has proven to be very successful. Group members perceive it as special permission to break the silence. Usually after a period of discussion about the barriers to discussing the problem, a consensus would be established to bring up the actual problem.

At times, silence was tied directly to a sexual issue, either homosexual or heterosexual. All youngsters in mid- to late adolescence are coming to grips with the expression of their sexuality, and our group members were no exception. Since they lived together on a twenty-four-hour basis, the sexual struggle was to some degree intensified. In our group, there were two nonverbal clues that this theme was operating: when group members of the opposite sex began sitting next to each other, and when one member of the group, usually a male, was actively ignored by the other group members.

When the silence was related to a sexual issue, we tried to be sensitive, supportive, direct, and informative in our approach. The adolescents in our group were no different from other adolescents in their need to talk about sexuality with adults other than their parents. Our method of bringing up the sexual theme (after we were fairly sure it was the issue) was to make a statement like, "I can see that bringing up matters about sexual feelings is difficult, but that's an important area for us to be able to talk about in group."

Once the declaration was made that sexual issues were important and that the group was a safe place to discuss these matters, it became much easier to introduce the topic in subsequent sessions. If sexuality is not discussed in group, then the group therapy experience is filled with the same—often unspoken—prohibition about sexual behavior that adolescents experience in society at large.

As we began to discuss sexual issues in our group, we came to several important realizations. The adolescents had numerous misconceptions about masculinity and femininity and a great need for accurate information about contraception. Many of them revealed very painful experiences from their own lives about attempted or actual incestuous relationships. Again, our early successes in being able to discuss sexual concerns openly with group members led to very meaningful sessions later.

SCAPEGOATING

As our group began to master the resistance of silence, another resistance emerged that is common to all groups. In our group's development, scapegoating was a pervasive theme for several sessions, and we learned a great deal about our group and ourselves in handling it.

According to Toker (1972), scapegoating is an essential group happening, and this proved to be especially true for our adolescent group. The first time it emerged, the ingredients included a higher than usual level of anxiety, hostility, and frustration about how the group was progressing and being led, and about the entry of a new member.

The new member was a fifteen-year-old girl who looked about thirteen. Elizabeth was very overweight and looked like a prepubertal child. She dressed seductively and wore an excessive amount of makeup. Her behavior in group was anxiety-ridden, and she was somewhat awkward in dealing with the other group members.

After three sessions, the other girls began to criticize Elizabeth about her clothes, makeup, and the way she sat in group. Initially, she seemed to enjoy the attention she was receiving because in earlier sessions she had been ignored by both the boys and the girls in the group. But her initial delight was short-lived as the other girls became more and more angry with her, making comments such as, "You look like a damn slut," and "Why the hell don't you act fifteen; you act like a baby." To our amazement, Elizabeth would not defend herself but began crying like an eight- or nine-year-old.

Since this was the first time we had seen such intense scapegoating in our group, we were tempted to simply call a halt to the verbal attacks and let them know as gently as possible that this behavior was off limits. We waited a few minutes, and then intervened in a way that proved to be very useful. We became fascinated by the process of scapegoating and began to explore what was happening.

We entered into the process by asking questions of the group member who was doing most of the verbal attacking. One of our questions was, "What is it about her that makes you so upset?" The response was, "It's the damn way she is." The other therapist inquired, "Does she remind you of someone you had difficulty dealing with before?" Another group member added, "She just doesn't act her age. She's like my sister, a real pain in the ass." One therapist reflected, "In some ways her being immature is hard to look at and live with."

As one of us worked with Elizabeth, the other worked supportively with the other group members. This process allowed us to keep the scapegoating theme in focus, but in a somewhat more manageable form.

It turned out that Elizabeth had held the same image in her family and at school before her hospitalization. That she was a scapegoat in our group clearly demonstrated that this was a powerful recurring role for her. As this information emerged, the other members seemed fascinated about what they had learned about scapegoating. Their anger diminished, and they developed some constructive approaches to helping Elizabeth. Several girls decided to coach her about her dress, makeup, and behavior with boys. These efforts paid off to some degree, and in subsequent sessions she did not take up the role of scapegoat. In situations concerning the boys, however, the role was fixed, and they would not give it up as easily as the girls had.

In retrospect, we saw the scapegoating process as an essential building block. If we had intervened to prevent it, it could have stifled the growth and development of our adolescent group. We were careful not to let the scapegoating process get out of hand, however, but began to examine the motivation and the social and emotional dimensions. This exploration yielded valuable data for all the group members.

ACTING OUT

Progressing through the various resistances, we came to a period in the program during which it was almost impossible to continue. As more adolescents were screened and admitted to the unit, the group grew to ten members, and as the group grew, so did the number of episodes of acting out. Few interventions helped stabilize the group. We felt devalued as co-therapists and more like wardens than therapists.

On the surface, the acting out seemed to be powered by three factors. The therapy room was crowded, and most of the group members were boys who had a history of acting out prior to hospitalization. A senior member who had been fairly cooperative in the past now appeared to be manifesting a strong negative leadership style, both in the unit and in the group. Negative leadership or acting out seemed to be a tension release, particularly around feelings of intimacy or closeness in the group. It also seemed to be a recapitulation of defiance used with parents and teachers in the past.

This was a rather bleak period for us. We felt that some progress had been made, and now we perceived that the group was back at a rather primitive, disorganized level. It did not feel as if we were part of a group therapy process.

After one particularly painful session, we began to consider several possible solutions to our situation. First we considered simply waiting out this stormy period but rejected this option because, in a sense, we had been using a deferment approach and the group had continued to deteriorate. And by delaying, we were supporting behavior that was not in the group's best interest and had the potential to be dangerous to them and to us.

Another option we debated was to dismiss the senior group member who was modeling the negative leadership style, after a series of confrontations about his negative influence on the group. But we realized that if we used this approach, we ran the risk of a boycott by the members who strongly identified with him.

Finally, we pondered whether we should take a recess, rescreen the members, and start all over. Terminating the group at this point was not very attractive to us because it would be admitting that the group was not manageable.

We decided that designing another format would lessen the acting out, keep the group therapy program going, and avoid the potentially negative consequences of terminating a group member.

MODIFIED FISHBOWL FORMAT

We were aware that other therapists working with adolescents had experimented with modifications of the traditional group psychotherapy approach. These new procedures had taken into consideration the adolescent developmental process as well as what had previously proven successful in working with adolescents in group.

A number of researchers have used various formats, techniques, and group compositions to achieve specific goals with their adolecent populations. Rachman and Heller (1976), Goodman (1967), and Hamburg and Verenhorst (1972) had successfully used a self-help peer counseling format that included the use of popular music as a catalyst in group therapy for teenagers. Corder et al. (1977) used a therapeutic game specifically designed for adolescent group therapy. The content of the game dealt with significant issues in the adolescent developmental process. Fine, Knight-Webb, and Breau (1976) had used volunteer adolescent group members to act as models to help facilitate verbalizations in adolescent groups, with successful results.

Other writers and researchers had stressed the importance of using extensive peer modeling procedures with adolescents (Fine, Knight-Webb, and Vernon, 1977; Bandura, 1969; and Stumphauzer, 1976).

In a literature review, we came across several articles that addressed the training of adolescent group therapists, and the effects of observers on the process of group therapy (Bloom and Dobie, 1969).

Berkovitz and Sugar (1976) reported that the observation of ongoing therapy has been one of the most effective methods of teaching group therapy. In their article they cited various observation arrangements that had been used, such as observers sitting in the same room but apart from the group, or watching the group from behind a one-way mirror.

Yalom (1970) described a procedure in which group psychotherapy trainees observed a therapy group through a one-way mirror and then reversed roles with group members, permitting the patients to observe the therapist and trainees discussing what had taken place in the group session.

Berkovitz and Sugar varied and extended this format with a group of adolescents. In their procedure, the trainees observed behind a one-way mirror and then met with group members at the end of the session to process what had taken place. With the implementation of this format, they reported benefits to the participants and observers in the form of increased awareness, stimulation, and therapeutic impact.

For our adolescent group we modified and extended the Berkovitz and Sugar technique into a "modified fishbowl format," which included both an observation and a participation group. As in the procedure used by Berkovitz and Sugar, both groups met together at the end of each group session to process what had transpired in the observed group.

Our adolescents were involved in both the observation and participation groups. The therapists determined the group to which each adolescent was assigned on a session-by-session basis. Our goal with this new format was not to train adolescent group therapists but to make the group therapy a more meaningful and therapeutic experience for the adolescents.

As mentioned earlier, when the group reached ten members, various antitherapeutic group norms developed. Although historically the group had incorporated new members fairly easily, old members were now repeatedly reminiscing about how the group used to be, and they were doing little to make new members feel welcome, with comments like, "It's getting crowded in here," "It's a full house today," "Standing room only," and "I won't have a chance to talk today." Actually, there *was* less time per member for participation, and members often complained that they were not unable to establish closure adequately within the fifty-minute session. This was frustrating to members and led them to avoid issues involving significant feelings.

Consequently, instead of indoctrinating new members to healthy therapeutic norms, old members facilitated the development of pathological group norms. These included overt coalitions, with old members attacking and scapegoating new members; coalitions against the therapists; individuals talking to neighbors instead of listening to others; the use of the group as a "joke hour"; obvious reluctance to talk about major issues of therapeutic significance; and outright ridicule of any group member actively sabotaging and interrupting the group process to draw attention to himself.

Since extending group times was not administratively possible, we made various attempts, with limited success, to process the problem and resolve it within the current group context before we elected to bring up the modified fishbowl format with the group members.

In attempting to restructure the group in response to the problems, we discussed with the adolescents the option of forming two groups. It was suggested that one group could be more behaviorally focused, learning to control impulses, listen, and promote self-expression, and could perhaps serve as a pre-group-therapy experience, with the option of moving into the other, more advanced group. This proposal raised serious concern among the members that the group might be split into a "bright" group and a "dull" group. There was also a fear that if the two-group format were implemented, the population of the unit would be split, preventing certain relationships from developing, and specific conflicts from being negotiated. These factors motivated us to try the modified fishbowl technique, to which the group responded favorably, preferring this format to being separated into two distinct groups.

The traditional fishbowl procedure had successfully been used with various groups for many years as a microdiscussion and decision-making technique. Normally in this type of group, some of the members are placed in a center group to discuss questions, while the other members sit around them and listen. After a certain amount of time, the outer group comes into the center and discusses the same questions or a different issue. Sometimes a "tap-in" procedure is used to allow those on the outside to express their views directly. A fishbowl-type format has helped groups move over roadblocks in the decision-making process and has allowed all group members to participate more easily (Napier and Gersehnfeld, 1973).

We implemented the modified fishbowl format in the regular interview format, with five group members observing behind the one-way mirror. At the beginning of each session, the therapists divided the larger group into participants and observers, with the latter being instructed to go behind the one-way mirror with a third therapist to observe the group.

Each group session lasted fifty minutes, with the participants spending thirty-five to forty minutes in group discussion while the observers looked on. The last ten to fifteen minutes were spent in group process, with the observers joining the participants and commenting on what they discerned during the group. The group members' reactions and feelings were dealt with at that time.

Initially, we hoped this format would serve several functions in regard to both the participants' and the observers' experiences. We thought the smaller participant group would foster more relevant participation, allow for better closure of each session, decrease competition, allow therapists to separate disruptive dyads, and decrease the need, as well as the opportunity, for interruptions and diversions from significant issues.

In addition, we predicted that the observational experience would serve a behavioral learning function that could be particularly helpful to the less verbal, more impulsive or inhibited members, without the disadvantage of splitting the different types of adolescents into two separate groups. There were certain behavior expectations, it was hypothesized, inherent in the observer role, including listening, reflecting, identifying others' feelings, and learning about group process and purpose, with the help of the third therapist. We anticipated that once these behaviors were learned in the observer role, which produced less anxiety, they would then generalize to the adolescents' behavior in the participant group. We also speculated that the observation experience might allow enough distance to desensitize some members to the idea of talking about feelings and making personal disclosures. In addition, we felt that objective peer feedback could perhaps more easily occur from the observer standpoint and that this feedback could serve as a valuable resource for the participant group.

The role of the third therapist was an essential element in the efficiency of the observer group. This therapist, who had functioned previously as an observer-supervisor, now encouraged the observing adolescents to join him in the role of consultant, eliciting their perceptions and sharing his own. The therapist asked questions of the observing adolescents, such as, "What do you think is going on with Joe?"; "Why do you suppose Rich changed the subject?"; "Who's the leader in the group?"; "Have you ever felt that way?"; and "What feeling does the group have?"

These questions led to responses such as, "I think he's angry and doesn't know it," "Nobody wants to talk about the real thing," "Brian's trying to control all of them by talking and everybody else is angry," "I think he's sad about his grandfather; I remember when my uncle died," "Everyone seems down," and "Everyone's picking on Jack."

Through such discussions, the observing therapist essentially moved the adolescents into looking at behavior, identifying feelings and defenses, understanding the relationship between feelings and behavior, identifying group themes and stages, and, in general, learning about group processes.

Another essential element of the third therapist's role was the coaching of the observers in giving constructive feedback, an important group skill. Before the group reconvened for the last ten or fifteen minutes, the third therapist discussed with the observers how they would present input in an honest but nonthreatening way.

Upon joining the interview group, each observer and the third therapist had an opportunity to discuss their reactions, with the group processing these remarks. Frequently, the participant group therapists consulted with the observers to seek assistance in defining a problem or to find a solution to a problem or block that had occurred during the session.

This new format generally succeeded in meeting the predicted goals and in facilitating some additional gains that had not been anticipated. Shortly after the implementation of the modified fishbowl format, the individuals in the participant group began talking about therapeutically significant issues such as relationship and identity problems, significant losses, and relationships with parents, and giving constructive feedback to each other, which they had previously avoided.

Initially, the suggestions were usually more objective, emphatic, and straightforward when given from the nonparticipating standpoint of the observer. Disruptive and scapegoating behavior, which had seemed fun or humorous, was seen in a less favorable light when observed from behind the mirror. Comments such as, "Things sure look different from the other side" or "You guys were acting silly" were frequently heard from the observers. This resulted in a decrease in disruptive behavior.

It also seemed that after being helped to identify the relationship between feelings and behavior in others, members became more comfortable with looking at the meaning of their own behavior, which led to more personal disclosures and empathetic statements. In summary, dysfunctional norms began to be replaced with healthier, therapeutic ones, with individuals manifesting better listening and processing skills and sharing appropriate feedback.

In addition to the predicted changes, some additional unanticipated benefits were noted. Because the composition of the smaller participant group changed from session to session, individuals had to adapt to a new grouping arrangement each time. Several individuals began exhibiting leadership behaviors they had not displayed before.

It also became possible to use the adolescents' experience as observers when they were in the participating group. The therapist might ask, for example, "What would you think if you were an observer today?" This enabled some participants to take a more objective view of their own behavior in the participant group, essentially allowing ego monitoring skills to be practiced.

The main factors operating in the behavior changes were the demand characteristics of being in both the participant and observer roles, and the modified fishbowl format was instrumental in initiating and directing many of these behavior changes. We did not collect hard data; the temporal sequence of the group members' changes in behavior coincided with the format changes.

The modified fishbowl format was not seen as a panacea for disruptive or chaotic group behavior but simply as a tool to facilitate a change in the group's direction. It enabled us to organize the group in a way that fostered more productive behaviors and allowed more positive leadership styles to emerge. This format was used as a temporary mechanism to facilitate the development of healthy therapeutic norms, with the option of reconvening the regular group once these norms were established; after ten sessions, the group elected to return to the original format.

After returning to one group, we held a lengthy discussion about the modified fishbowl format. The members felt it had increased their interest in coming to group, and they were now more unified as a result of the experience. We felt the group had become more cohesive and now had the strength to deal with difficult issues in the future, decreasing the need, as well as the opportunity, for interruptions and diversions from significant issues.

SUMMARY

In the selected review of techniques used in adolescent group therapy, it is clear that group therapists have successfully used videotaping, nonverbal exercises, poetry, therapeutic games, and behavioral techniques to facilitate communication and to overcome specific resistances.

Using this information, we designed various techniques to meet the specific problems that emerged in our group. Our model demanded that as resistances such as testing the co-therapists, withdrawal, and silence came to the surface, we had to develop techniques in response to them. At a point when the group appeared to be on the verge of disintegrating, we designed the modified fishbowl technique, with the result that we were able to continue and move to a higher level of functioning.

6

TRANSITION PHASE

> A moment's insight is worth a life's experience.
>
> —Oliver Wendell Holmes, Sr.
> *The Professor at the Breakfast-Table*

In this chapter the group continues the process of personal growth, moving from counterdependence and flight to an exploration of self and others, learning to better monitor one's own behaviors and those of other group members, and, perhaps most important, learning to express feelings accurately.

GAINS FROM THE MODIFIED FISHBOWL TECHNIQUE

The modified fishbowl technique was a much more powerful intervention than we realized when we implemented it. It immediately increased our confidence; we had weathered a very stormy period in the group's development. Our anxiety had diminished considerably and we were no longer feeling the anger, resentment, and confusion we had felt during that difficult acting-out time. We had survived a period where other groups stop functioning altogether or simply continue in an atmosphere of chronic resistance, without ever moving to a more positive level.

Our new self-confidence helped us engage the group members in a more meaningful way. Recognizing that we had passed through a difficult period of primitive resistances and group regression, we made a commitment to each other that we would do everything possible in future sessions not to let the group move back to the previous dysfunctional level. We were prepared to react more effectively if individuals or the group as a whole began to move toward withdrawal, avoidance, or lack of control.

INCREASED SELF-DISCLOSURE

After the fishbowl intervention, we experienced a dramatic shift in the group members' behavior. There was very little acting out, withdrawal, or complaining about unit staff, teachers, or individual therapists. The group members, for the first time, began to engage in self-disclosure, presenting material that was very pertinent to them as youngsters in midadolescence. They revealed concerns about sexual struggles, school performance, peer relationships, problems with parents, their own suffering in growing toward adulthood, and what it meant to them to be psychiatric patients.

The disclosure of this material indicated that our members saw the group as a safe place to bring up significant material and concerns. We speculated that this peception was related to their mastery of the chaotic phase of the group's development. Possibly the adolescents saw us as persevering with them during the worst of times; consequently, since we met the test, we could be trusted to work with them on real issues. We experienced the group members as more accepting of us and our commitment to help them.

It also seemed as if they were going to allow us to be supportive of them and that they knew our role was a difficult one. We felt closer to the group members and to each other as co-therapists, and the group atmosphere was characterized by more understanding and liking of each other. All these factors played a key role in increasing the level of self-disclosure that began to take place.

NEW RESISTANCES

As the content moved into important adolescent themes, a new set of more sophisticated resistances appeared on the scene. A group member would bring up an important issue, such as his struggles with sexual feelings, and after proceeding briefly would become quite anxious and stop talking. At other times, group members would prematurely shut down the initiating one with comments like, "You shouldn't feel that way" or "I can't believe you do that" or "I don't think that you should bring that up."

We realized that the content was at a level of complexity and emotion beyond the group's capacity to process it. The material had advanced faster than our ability to deal with it. This caused us a great deal of anxiety. We felt the group members were finally running risks in presenting meaningful material, but we did not have the resources operating to process that information effectively. We needed to design an intervention that would quickly enable the group to become effective in processing the rich material being presented.

Our approach needed to respect the group members' risk taking in disclosing important material and at the same time not move them toward power struggles and control issues experienced in the past. What we soon developed and implemented was a technique that helped maintain and enhance the members' self-disclosure and prevented power struggles and regressive episodes.

CO-THERAPIST DIALOGUE

Our strategy was an elaboration of an approach used during an earlier phase of the group's development. In the past, whenever we experienced a direct control issue within the group, ranging from aggressive, provocative behavior to passive refusal to participate, and when direct interventions or confrontations evoked more of the same resistant behavior, one of us would elaborate on how we felt we were in a double bind in dealing with the specific resistance. In that double bind, we had two poor or negative options: to collude in the behavior by not confronting it or to confront it and provoke more of the same.

In the past our confrontations or interpretations had the potential of escalating into overt power struggles, which often reinforced the adolescents' negative view of authority and justified further provocation on their part. At this point we were not faced with provocative behavior or withdrawal. The problem we faced was that many important topics were shut down without being fully explored or processed effectively. We therefore reintroduced the procedure of posing the operating dilemma through our co-therapist dialogue.

For example, when one member, Mike, was cut off from talking about his struggles with his parents by another group member, one co-therapist turned to the other and said, "You know, when Mike talks about his parents, I get the feeling that in many ways he's been overly protected, and even smothered, and has been unable to grow up in his family. At the same time, I feel his extreme sense of responsibility for them, his need to protect them, and to avoid in any way having an opinion which they see as different, and that this has become quite a struggle for him; that's why I believe he has these periods of confusion, or as he calls them, 'craziness,' when he cannot function on his own. This is perhaps his way of not having to deal with the ways in which he disagrees with them. I think maybe he is overprotecting them the way they overprotect him. Yet I am concerned that if I should say this to him that I would be being too intrusive and would put him in the position of having to protect them even more. What do you think?'' The other co-therapist would then agree, add interpretations or offer a different view, or we would check our perceptions with members of the group or with the adolecent himself.

In some ways the dialogue resembles what is often called collaboration, or consultation, which we usually did outside the group for the primary purpose of planning treatment. By incorporating this aspect of collaboration into the group sessions and by making the adolescents observers to these discussions, additional functions were served.

First, we found that more therapeutic material could be introduced with this more oblique, less direct approach. This type of dialogue between co-therapists ordinarily demanded no response from the adolescent, who was free to listen and was often fascinated by the discussion. As a matter of fact, when we first introduced the co-therapist dialogue, the group members were very positive about the approach. It was as if they had never seen adults who were interested and struggling with material presented by an adolescent. Most of them commented that their parents never talked the way we were talking to each other.

Some of them felt good that we could get at the dilemmas and help them get unstuck without a lot of negative things happening. When one girl became upset about our co-therapist dialogue and asked us not to talk that way because it made her very uncomfortable, we investigated her concern and found out she had lived with a fantasy that adults, including her parents, talked negatively and in an uncaring way when she was not around. After we worked with her on this problem, she became a big fan of the co-therapist dialogue technique.

When we made a direct interpretation to an adolescent and demanded a response, we discovered that most of them found it difficult, if not impossible, to respond. It often raised resistances even before the explanation was complete, since they felt placed in a position in which they must confirm or reject material. The indirect approach of the co-therapist dialogue, on the other hand, often made it easier for the adolescent to hear the material, reflect on it, or incorporate it. Just as our observing adolescents often saw more from behind the mirror than when they were in the therapy room, this approach placed the adolescents behind an invisible mirror, making them observers to a caring therapeutic discussion about themselves.

The co-therapist dialogue implicitly placed the adolescent in a different role in the group. When a therapist was interacting directly with an adolescent, the other therapist was an observer who functioned as a consultant to that interaction. When one of us turned to the other to discuss an adolescent's dilemma, this put the adolescent in the role of being a consultant about himself, because the issue being discussed by the co-therapists had to do with him.

It was our experience that in this outside consultant role, adolescents were often likely to volunteer additional information about their dilemma, and the group would stay on the material longer than when an individual was confronted by other members or got a direct interpretation from one of the co-therapists. An additional benefit of these dialogues was that they greatly reduced the adolescents' fears that the therapists were discussing them behind their backs. Our technique introduced a level of candor and honesty that was very beneficial to the therapeutic process.

While many group therapists restrict direct feedback to their adolescent patients in an attempt to remain "neutral," we found that the adolescents in our group had interpreted our "neutrality" in the past as a lack of concern or acceptance. Moreover, our experience revealed that nondisclosure on our part, although at times an attempt to remain neutral, often gave us a kind of therapeutic power and did not allow the youngsters access to material that ultimately could be used for change. Disclosing more information about our thoughts and hypotheses actually reduced suspicion, created a cleared alliance between us and the group members, and conveyed the notion that any material, including the co-therapists' response, was available for discussion.

The co-therapist dialogue brought us closer together as a group, creating a greater depth of psychological intimacy than we had thought possible. An attitude began to emerge that we, as a group, were now equipped to deal with whatever material was brought up. Their interest had increased dramatically and seemed powered by our modeling of how to deal with complex personal issues without any catastrophic consequence. They saw us as competent adults trying to figure out how to look at human problems, and it soon became apparent that they wanted to do this themselves. We had, in essence, imitated healthy parenting of the group members. This stage marked the beginning of social competency development in terms of healthy self-parenting by the group members.

NEW BEHAVIORS IN THE GROUP

The co-therapist dialogue led to several changes in the group. The flexibility it afforded was mirrored in the group members as they dealt with each other and with us. For example, when issues were initiated, members would ask for more information in a supportive way instead of dismissing them out of hand. They would give supportive opinions about a particular issue or give concrete examples of how they had handled a similar situation. In some instances, one group member would talk to another about a problem involving a third member. This approach was very similar to the co-therapist dialogue and the consultation process.

Some group members even began to use the words "consultation" and "let's process it" within the context of the group. On numerous occasions, one group member would ask other members for a consultation about relationships with teachers they all had. Consultation about school ranged from group members not liking specific aspects of certain teachers' behavior to difficulties in learning a subject either because of the way it was taught or because the student didn't like the material. It was amazing how well this consultation process worked and how effectively the group members could get at the essence of a problem and then make some specific recommendation about how to solve it.

The capacity to process complex content in the group was magnificent to behold. As competency continued to develop, members began to comment on the group's development as an entity. One member said, "Remember when we had to go behind the one-way mirror because everything was out of contol here?" Other comments included, "Boy, things are much better in group now" and "I like coming to group because we get something done."

The adolescents began to see that each of them had various roles to play in the group, and these roles were openly discussed. They referred to group members who sat in a specific chair as sitting in the "hot seat," a reference to a period when a person wanting to initiate a topic sat in a specific chair during a session. They referred to the process of rescuing a group member from a difficult situation as "life boat" and the person doing the saving as a "rescuer." They saw others as "rule makers" and "rule breakers."

At times when the group was struggling, some of the members called on another member they thought could be a "facilitator." For example, the members we saw as "listeners" were often called on to clarify what was going on in terms of the growth process; the "rule maker" was sometimes called on to comment about the fairness of how a particular issue was being transacted.

Instead of backing off from certain problems, the group began to feel challenged by specific content that was disclosed and seemed fascinated by how to process difficult problems. One such instance centered around a sexual theme. At the beginning of one group session, a group member, John, announced he had something to bring up that was bothering him. Without much difficulty we established that the issue was in the sexual area, but then he became extremely anxious, even though we were all very supportive, both directly and in a dialogue with each other. His nonverbals suggested that this sensitive issue was not going to be disclosed fully without some strong reassurances.

At this point his fellow group members asked him why he was so worried about bringing his problem up in group. His response was, "If I tell you, none of you will ever speak to me again." So we knew that in part his anticipation of peer rejection was powering his refusal to go further with his self-disclosure. The members processed his concern about their potential rejection of him and achieved a consensus that they would not reject him, no matter what his problem happened to be. We reaffirmed that whatever he said would be OK with us and that we would not think badly of him.

Even with all these reassurances, John remained reluctant to discuss his problem. Finally, he announced that he could talk to the male co-therapist about the issue, but could not open up in front of the female co-therapist and group members. One of the adolescents asked if he could talk about it with the male co-therapist if the others went behind the one-way mirror. After about a minute, John said, "I think so." The female co-therapist and the rest of the group then asked him what he wanted them to do as observers after he talked with the male co-therapist. He said he didn't know. We eventually agreed to talk about what he revealed as much as he was comfortable with, once the observers came back in the room.

Everyone left the room, except John and the male co-therapist. Without much prompting, he began to describe in detail how he became sexually excited when he touched women's undergarments, and disclosed that he masturbated with underwear belonging to his mother and sister. After this disclosure, he seemed quite guilt-ridden but relieved that he had finally told someone about it. The male co-therapist told that he understood how difficult it was for him to bring this problem up, but was glad that he felt safe enough to finally begin to get it worked on in group.

After a brief period, John indicated that the observers could come back into the room. As the group reassembled, a moderate amount of anxiety manifested itself, and the male members quickly began to be very supportive. One boy said, "I'll bet you're glad to get that off your chest." Another said, "Hey, way to go." Others said, "No big thing" and "Don't sweat it."

The girls were noticeably quiet, and the female co-therapist asked them how they felt about what they had heard. One girl said, "It sounds like a hard problem for him to deal with." "I never thought guys would do stuff like that." As the group ended, John received more reassurance from the males that they would not reject him.

We commended the group for how effectively they had dealt with the disclosure and pointed out that earlier our group would not have been able to handle the issue. Finally, we asked John if he felt better and if we had done enough work on the problem for the time being. He said we had.

After the group, we talked with each other about how powerful this particular session had been. The amount of effort and caring about John's problem, and the cooperation, planning, and support in working through this tough issue, were very touching to us. We had a sense of being present in a competent, caring peer group of youngsters in mid-adolescence who had a tremendous capacity to care for one of their own.

NEW BEHAVIORS OUTSIDE THE GROUP

We wondered if the new level of interpersonal competency being demonstrated in the group sessions was being used in other facets of the adolescents' lives. This question was soon answered as they shared examples of how they coped with problems outside of the group. These usually centered around dilemmas with their individual therapists, parents, or peers.

One male group member, Bob, talked about how he handled his problem of talking frankly with his father. Bob had a long history of getting into violent arguments with his father about his appearance, rules in the family, and his academic work. On a weekend pass from the hospital, without any preparation from the group, he decided to initiate contact with his father before they became involved in an argument. He told his father that he had learned to talk with adults differently in the hospital and that he wanted to try talking with him the way he did with the doctors.

The father, as Bob reported, initially did not want anything to do with the approach, but his wife encouraged him to listen, and the process of contact began with all members of the family present. Bob told his father that he wanted a different relationship with him and not to be fighting all the time.

As we listened to his report in group, it became clear that Bob was really, in a sense, parenting his father. He revealed that they admitted to each other how they had not shown mutual respect in the past and that their fights had been attempts to get back at each other. Other members of Bob's family clarified aspects of the father-son conflict and also began to confess that they did not help when the dissension was really bad. All of these accounts certainly had the flavor of family therapy without an official family therapist being present.

Another group member, a girl who had been attending public high school outside the hospital, reported a very important peer interaction. Margaret had been going to school near the hospital as part of her preparation for outpatient status. One day at lunch, a student asked in a very confrontational manner why she was attending a school outside the hospital. As Margaret began to explain her treatment program, the other student said, "That's a bunch of shit." Margaret replied, "Wait a minute, I want to process something with you."

The other students were interested in this approach to peer interaction and became absorbed in hearing what Margaret had to say. She told them how difficult it was to be in the hospital and attending an outside school. She described how she had learned a great deal about herself and how to get along with others while in the hospital and how she was anxious to get out.

Our group members cheered her courageous and forthright approach in this trying situation. And Margaret now had a support group at school. The positive response in group was not only for her effective handling of the situation, but for the sense it gave the other members that they could manage their own eventual reentry into school after their hospitalization.

Another girl, Ann, revealed to us that things had improved dramatically in her individual therapy once she had confronted her therapist about his lack of interest and confidence in her. Ann was perhaps one of the most sensitive and psychologically minded adolescents we had in our program. She explained to her therapist that she needed a give-and-take in therapy and that his inactivity bothered her and left her feeling cheated. She said that she was shaking inside when she told her therapist how she felt about him, but it made sense for her to do it. As a result, things were much better now in her individual therapy and she liked her therapist much more. This report immediately led the other group members to discuss their relationships with their individual therapists.

These personal testimonies about how difficult situations were being handled outside of group were a tremendous source of encouragement to the group members who were less confident. As individual members became more competent inside and outside of group, they became positive peer leaders and, in a sense, peer therapists.

THERAPISTS AS REFLECTORS

The transition phase seemed almost like the beginning of a "golden era" in our group's development. As the group members changed, so did we as therapists, as we reflected on the competency that had developed in the group. We all expressed our belief the group was functioning much better and at a higher level, giving concrete examples of how we all listened more attentively to each other, gave excellent feedback, and demonstrated genuine care for each other.

Relieved of the burdensome role of the past, we became less anxious about energizing the group when it slowed down, or cutting off minor regressive episodes that might move the group back to a lower level of functioning. We trusted ourselves to trust the process of therapy, and this was a major turning point in our work as group therapists and the overall movement of the group. There developed a meaningful level of intimacy in the group. We all seemed very much in synchronization with each other; resistance and control maneuvers were at a minimum and empowerment of each other became the main theme.

During this period we would compliment members directly when we saw them engaged in healthy, socially competent behaviors. For example, when a member who had usually been very shy and quiet in group started talking more, we commented, "We've always experienced you in group as quiet, and we feel real good seeing the talkative side of you." A member who had always presented a rather tough posture about issues and who became very tender and sensitive with another group member in one session received the response, "We've seen how strong you've been in group but we're impressed today by your sensitivity and tenderness." A group member who usually related in a confused manner appeared very organized and assertive in one session, to which we responded, "Today in group we experienced you as very clear and strong about dealing with that issue."

The group members were very accepting of our precise feedback. Recognizing new behaviors in the group members quickly became part of the group culture, and our members stopped giving the superficial, controlling type of compliments they had used with each other in the past.

As this golden era continued, an interesting shift occurred regarding the group members' relationship with us. The adolescents became very interested in our personal lives. Some asked if we were married and had children, others asked if we were single and dated each other. One member wanted to know if we used drugs, and if we did not, how we could understand someone with a drug problem.

It soon became apparent we were in a new period of testing. There was a sense that we had perhaps become too close to the group members and they wanted to, at one level, make us fully like them and, at another level, move us back into a more formalized therapy role. Our immediate clinical intuition told us not to give their questions factual answers.

When we redirected their questions with responses like, "How come it's important to know that about us?" one group member said, "Tell us what we asked you, 'cause you know everything about us." We became aware that some group members felt as if they had shared more specific content about their lives than we had as therapists.

Again we moved back to the issue of what purpose it would serve for them to have a great deal of detailed information about us. We explained that in a real sense, if we talked about ourselves and our personal lives, that would stop therapy from happening, because in therapy it is important to be free to wonder about the therapist. In friendships outside of group, we recognized that it was important to get to know everything one could about a new friend; therapy relationships, on the other hand, were more powerful in some ways than friendships.

At this point the group member who had instigated the personal questions began to laugh. He revealed that he was glad we did not answer the questions with facts and said all he really wanted was to see how we would handle this type of situation. We asked him if we passed the test, and he smilingly responded, "You sure did."

SUMMARY

This period in the life of our group was very special, and in one sense we believed we had come to the apex of therapy with the adolescents. The contrast between the early difficulties in group, the false starts and the regressive episodes with the primitive resistances, seemed an unpleasant part of our group's distant history. The present situation in group was so rich and exciting therapeutically that we did not anticipate the maturing process of our group to continue with future sessions.

7

DEALING WITH CHANGES IN THE GROUP

The first step toward solving a problem is to begin.

—Anonymous

Our focus in this chapter is on dealing with change. This is one of the most difficult aspects for group members. If life remained relatively stable, the learning and the teaching would be considerably simplified. Members would not have to deal with new members who are just beginning the therapy process with their limited insight and nonadaptive behaviors. They would not lose their friends from the group who supported them in periods of stress. Finally, members would not have to deal with staff changes or their own departure from the group.

In this phase of our group's development, it began functioning in a special way when new members were added. The older members seemed to want to preserve the safety and freedom of the group and not have it disturbed by new members coming in or old members leaving.

Since the reality of our situation was that some members would always be leaving and others would always be coming in, we needed to establish specific tactics or rituals that would address the entry and departure of group members actively and directly. These rituals, while initiated by us, were really developed and enriched by all the group members.

It also became important at this stage to incorporate a trainee therapist, so one co-therapist left the group and became an observer therapist. This shift required the development of another set of tactics.

These newly established strategies were developed to prevent major regressions in the group's functioning. We knew that regression occurs every time a group's membership changes; we felt strongly, however, that the process could be managed so the group would not move back to a less sophisticated level of functioning. We also saw an opportunity in the arrival and departure of group members for the discussion of acceptance-rejection and separation-individuation themes.

PREPARING FOR NEW MEMBERS

Because we screened all the adolescent inpatients on the unit who were referred for group therapy, the members of our group understood that we made the final determination about who came to therapy. Before a new member entered the group, old members were informed and given an opportunity to process and resolve their resistance regarding the acceptance of the new member. To some degree we were using the old members as consultants about the new member.

Once we announced a new member's arrival, the old members would usually respond with negative comments like, ''He's too weird,'' or ''She won't fit in.'' We learned not to evaluate or cut short their negative statements, believing it important for them to get out all the negative feelings before the new member arrived. We listened to the comments and at times were curious and even fascinated about the basis for their concerns, but we were never critical or rejecting of their opinions.

Sometimes we asked the group members to fantasize about how a particular problem might be handled with a new member. The fantasy exercise proved to be a very potent tactic and was a good indicator of how a new member would do in group. As our discussion about the member became more positive, we would focus on what resources we had that might benefit him or her. Eventually, the group would be discussing ways in which the new member would profit from the group, and this type of discussion set the stage for his or her acceptance.

TACTICS FOR INCORPORATING NEW MEMBERS INTO THE GROUP

When an adolescent entered our group, we systematically did several things in order to make him or her feel at home. Both of us would welcome this new member to the group with ''I'm very glad you're here in group with us,'' or ''It's real nice to have you as a new member of our group.'' This unambivalent greeting modeled our method of acceptance for the members of the group and gave our endorsement to the usually anxious new member.

Next, we asked the new member show he or she wanted to be addressed. For instance, if her name was Elizabeth, we would ask if she preferred to be called Elizabeth or Liz. Our experience in group had taught us that adolescents were very sensitive about how they were addressed by us as well as by their peers.

We would then ask an old member to formally orient the new member about the way the group worked. As this transpired, the group's norms or rules were usually reaffirmed, and the process of incorporating the new member started. Sometimes group norms that were vague became more precise, and sometimes implicit rules were articulated for the first time. It was helpful if one of the more powerful group members participated actively in the orientation because this would lend a sense of positive peer sponsorship to the new member.

During this initial session, we generally asked the new member to describe briefly why he had come to the hospital, his family background, and problems he was working on in therapy. This request was usually not too difficult for the new member because he had talked about the same material in the screening interview.

Although there were a few exceptions, it was usually very important in this initial session for the new member to make some disclosures of a fairly personal nature in order to invest something of value in the group. This process broke the ice for the new member and helped to bring him to the level of personal disclosure that had been operating in the group prior to his arrival.

In some respects the new member's disclosures decreased regression in the group. New members usually anticipated and were prepared to make some self-disclosures during the initial session; if this did not happen, their reluctance to share information increased rather than decreased over subsequent sessions, enhancing the likelihood of significant overall group regression.

Usually the entire session was spent greeting, orienting, and listening to the new member. This process was never hurried, and a great effort was made to incorporate him fully into the group. At the end of this initial session, we would check with the new member about how he felt about his first hour, asking if he had any additional questions about any aspect of the group. Before breaking up, we would again tell him how glad we were that he had joined our group, and often some of the adolescents would verbalize their positive feelings about him being there.

Taking time to prepare for a new member and to incorporate him into the group during the initial session promoted a great deal of individual social competency and served to prevent major regressions in group functioning.

OLD MEMBERS LEAVING THE GROUP

Just as the process of incorporating a new member proved to be significant, the loss of an old member was also a very powerful experience in the group. Many of our adolescents had histories of frequent and disruptive life changes, including upheavals in family relationships, school placements, and peer relationships. All of our group members had experienced interpersonal losses that were abrupt, painful, and conflictual. They had suffered a great deal of trauma in the area of personal loss, and we did not want to have a group process that replicated these past traumas.

On the other hand, entering and exiting from relationships, including their group experience, was a natural and essential life experience in their movement toward mature adulthood. Our work on the process of transition provided them with a valuable opportunity to gain some mastery over past experiences and to develop a foundation, or model, for competently approaching new relationships and future losses.

TACTICS FOR SAYING GOOD-BYE

In our group we gave special significance to the termination process. When a group member announced that she was going to be discharged from the hospital by a specific date, we responded by building group consensus that some time in subsequent sessions would be devoted to discussing the member's departure. Over time, the group developed a specific structure for the last session attended by a departing group member, which eventually became incorporated into group therapy as an expected tradition.

Each group member, in turn, would talk directly with the departing member about the strengths and changes he or she had observed, how the member would be missed in the group, and any concerns, hopes, or fears about the member's future outside the hospital.

Often one of the therapists would go first in giving the feedback to the departing member and model the process, summing up special strengths the member had brought to the group, as well as identifying concerns or issues that needed continued work.

For example, one adolescent had been hospitalized for a severe drug-abuse problem, depression, and family conflicts. Our termination feedback with Larry was, "Larry, when you first started in group you were very quiet, and then you became active and one of the main leaders of the group. I liked your ability to help group members out with what they had to say and the emotional support you gave each member.

"I'm worried that if you start to go around with those same friends you had before coming in the hospital, you'll start to use drugs again. Also, I'm concerned that some of the major problems in your family are not worked out yet. I hope you and your family stay in family therapy once you leave the hospital."

This feedback, given with obvious care and concern, was offered in a tender and respectful manner and carried with it a sense of one human being caring about another. Larry's response to the feedback included the following comments: ''I've done a lot better the last couple of months in the hospital. I've been able to talk better with my therapist and here in group. I'm going to help my family in family therapy and at home with what I've learned in the hospital. I don't think my friends can get me to use drugs again like before I came in the hospital.''

Now each group member and the other therapist had the opportunity to give specific feedback to Larry. After everyone had completed his or her turn, Larry gave his feedback to all remaining members and the therapists, speaking directly to each of them.

A heightened degree of sensitivity often appeared during these termination sessions, facilitating greater depth of group interaction and lending the feedback greater impact. Important but previously undisclosed feelings and information were frequently made public during these sessions.

At times, a departing member would leave the group a ''gift'' by bringing up some critical issue that then became an important theme in future groups. For example, Larry said, ''I didn't work on my problems for the first four months in the hospital; it's only in the last two months that I've faced up to what's going on with me.'' Continuing this theme, he then turned toward a female group member and said, ''I don't think you're working on your problem, and maybe you'll end up getting out of the hospital without getting any better.'' The issue he raised was rich material to be processed in subsequent sessions.

The structure this format provided seemed to decrease the group's anxiety and reduce the tendency toward avoidance of the termination process, helping to ensure a healthy closure to relationships. The group often functioned at its most sophisticated level during these sessions, which seemed to partially offset the regressive effects of the change in membership.

Each adolescent in the group had an opportunity during the termination process to give caring, empathetic feedback, which was usually given in a very sensitive, gentle fashion. We were often touched by the warmth expressed by the group members during the termination process.

One exception, however, remains vividly in our minds. A fifteen-year-old, who had a history of being the scapegoat in group sessions, was leaving. Before her departure, she announced to the group that she had become pregnant during her hospitalization and had decided to keep the baby.

In the session devoted to her termination, the feedback had gone quite well until a borderline female in the group said, ''You're a slut bitch and I hope you and your goddamned baby both die in childbirth.'' This group member had initiated scapegoating episodes in earlier sessions.

After the attack, several group members confronted the attacker and accused her of being insensitive and cruel. To diffuse the situation, we intervened and completed the termination. The attack on the departing member obviously neutralized some of the benefits usually experienced by departing members. (Her attacker, later transferred back to a juvenile delinquency facility because she became unmanageable in our psychiatric setting, was subsequently charged with voluntary manslaughter after she ran over and killed three children.)

CO-THERAPISTS LEAVING: TACTICS FOR SAYING GOOD-BYE

When a co-therapist left the group, a similar set of tactics was initiated, with some modifications. As one therapist left, a new therapist was preparing to enter the group, so we needed to develop a format that incorporated both processes simultaneously.

Departing therapists usually initiated the termination process, dealing with the group members' feelings about their leave-taking over a period of several sessions. Therapists who leave a group abruptly and without time for their patients to deal with the pain of the departure are doing a major therapeutic disservice to their patients as well as themselves.

Prior to the final termination group session, the departing therapist invited the new therapist to the group for two sessions. Having the new therapist in the group allowed the group members to see the new therapist in the context of the therapy hour.

During these sessions, the departing therapist introduced the new therapist to the group and, in a sense, acted as a sponsor for the new therapist, with the expectation that this sponsorship would facilitate a transfer of power and function to the incoming therapist. The departing therapist would gradually become less active, deferring responsibility to the new therapist. We found that it was equally important during these sessions that the remaining co-therapist actively engage the new therapist and endorse the change. The new therapist did not attend the final termination session that followed these two transition sessions, allowing the departing therapist to leave in a more personal and private way.

The process of gently moving the new therapist in and the departing therapist out decreased the degree of regression in the group and allowed adequate termination to occur. This process also seemed to help resolve group members' concerns about loyalty to the departing therapist and promote a faster alliance with the new co-therapist.

PHASING IN A NEW CO-THERAPIST

Even with the format developed, we often found that it was difficult for the adolescents to give up a co-therapist who had spent considerable time in group with them. Themes centering around their feelings of loss and of not being able to give up their strong loyalty to their former therapist were allowed to surface and to be processed. Usually the co-therapist who had remained in the group played a major role in dealing with these issues.

The new co-therapist was not yet valued enough to deal with these themes and in some instances was scapegoated as causing the departure of the former co-therapist. Only time and proving oneself by dealing with difficult material would allow the new co-therapist to gain the power and status of the former co-therapist; a new co-therapist could not be imposed on the group.

SUMMARY

Even though the issues surrounding changes in the group were painful, the group reached a new level of functioning once these issues were addressed. Since we were no longer starting the group from scratch, there was a safety and freedom operating that allowed significant themes to be processed.

We began to explore the meaning of relationships, particularly parenting and dating, and examined what it meant to love someone. The group looked at loyalty as a value, and it looked at the meaning of other values related to peer and familial relationships. While earlier stages had seemed like a golden era, the emerging shape of our group proved to be a marvelous time of learning for all involved.

8

THEMES AND POSSIBLE CURATIVE FACTORS

Youth is to all the glad season of life: but often only by what it hopes, not by what it attains or what it escapes.

—Thomas Carlyle
Essays: Schiller

This chapter is devoted to exploring factors that may play a curative role in adolescent group therapy. Our initial focus is on the group itself in adolescent development. Next, we review self-disclosure in therapy groups and research on curative factors in therapy. Moving from the research literature, we consider the high level of functioning observed clinically in our own group.

GROUP ITSELF

Brockbank (1980) stressed that the importance of the group to the adolescent has been known by those who have observed and worked with children and youths for many years. He cited Erikson's (1968) studies of individual and group identity in adolescents, which have enabled theoreticians to conceptualize the factors that have made adolescent group formation such an essential aspect of adolescent developmental psychology.

We now recognize that group formation makes it possible for the adolescent to do a number of important things necessary for the resolution of certain conflicts that must be accomplished during this period of life. The adolescent achieves this conflict resolution in the group first through the displacement of much unresolved childhood dependency on parents onto the peer group. This displacement allows the beginning of decathexis of parents as the exclusive focus upon which infantile and latency conflicts are acted out.

This, of course, makes the adolescent peer group crucial for adolescent development. It also sets the stage for certain group dynamics to occur in the adolescent therapy group.

SELF-DISCLOSURE

Psychotherapists agree that in order for any form of psychotherapy to occur, a patient must reveal himself to a therapist. Much of this revelation occurs unwittingly, on both verbal and nonverbal levels, and this may form the basis of a substantial part of psychotherapy. This process of self-disclosure may in itself be a goal of therapy.

Jourard (1968) emphasized the importance of a capacity for self-disclosure in interpersonal relationships, arguing that self-disclosure maintains psychological health and fosters personal growth. It may also be seen as a necessary precondition for the implementation of various curative factors in group psychotherapy, according to Corsini and Rosenberg (1955) and Yalom (1970). For example, in the early stages of group, self-disclosure promotes universality by increasing members' awareness that their feelings and problems are not unique.

Perhaps most important, self-disclosure provides much of the basis of interpersonal learning; not only must members disclose information about themselves, but others must follow suit by disclosing their reactions to such information. From the point of view of self-disclosure as a goal, the group is a particularly useful modality. Compared to individual therapy, a group fosters self-disclosure in a wider and more representative social context, thus increasing the likelihood of generalization beyond the therapy situation.

CURATIVE FACTORS

Corder, Whiteside, and Haizlip (1981) cited Yalom's research on curative factors in group psychotherapy as providing the impetus for an increasing number of investigations of patients' perceptions of group conditions and experiences that promote positive changes.

From the research of Maxmen (1973) and Rohrbaugh and Bartels (1975), a tentative list of conditions and mechanisms within group has been hypothesized to promote behavior change, including altruism, group cohesiveness, universality, interpersonal learning (input and output), guidance, catharsis, identification, family reenactment, insight, instilling of hope, and existential awareness.

Corder et al. (1981) claimed that there is no literature that deals specifically with adolescents' perception of curative factors in group psychotherapy. In their research they used a Q-Sort of Yalom's description of potential curative factors in group psychotherapy with adolescents in four clinical settings: two in an outpatient mental health setting, one at a regional child guidance clinic, and one at a psychiatric training center. Membership included both outpatients and inpatients hospitalized for short-term treatment. All subjects in the research had attended groups for at least six months.

The adolescents reported that it was difficult to do the Q-sort, which is a tool for ranking traits or characteristics from "most like" to "least like." Still used occasionally by researchers, it was first described in the 1930s.

The sixteen adolescents, ranging in age from thirteen to seventeen, had to sort sixty cards containing the statements describing Yalom's curative factors in group psychotherapy. They were to place the cards into seven categories: most helpful to me in group, extremely helpful, very helpful, helpful, barely helpful, less helpful, and least helpful.

After the sorting, the adolescents were interviewed for fifteen to twenty minutes about their reasons for choosing the most helpful and least helpful items. Corder and her colleagues listed the items found to be most helpful and extremely helpful to the adolescents (Table 3) and those they chose as less helpful and least helpful (Table 4).

They found that adolescents and adults show some very similar patterns of perceptions of curative factors in group psychotherapy. In strikingly similar choices, the adolescents listed four of the five items ranked highest by adults as curative factors, which come from Yalom's catharsis, interpersonal learning, and existential factors categories. Adolescents and adults clearly differed on the insight category items. The adolescents, according to the study, gave high rankings to items describing aspects of group cohesiveness and universality, along with other categories related to the importance of interpersonal relationships among group members.

GROUP FUNCTIONING

We believe that most adolescent groups and many adult groups do not reach the level of functioning we experienced at times with our adolescent group. The themes produced in group on these occasions were extremely powerful, and the group skills used to process them were at an optimal level. In retrospect, it is difficult to identify all the factors that produced this level of group functioning, but we have some theories.

Our behavior certainly played a facilitating role in the group's cohesiveness. We maintained a consistent level of direct caring for the adolescents and continued to be openly self-expressive. Active listening,

Table 3
Items Most Helpful and Extremely Helpful to Adolescents

Item	Category	Percentage	Item Statement
7-35*	Catharsis	44	Being able to say what was bothering me instead of holding it in
7-34*	Catharsis	38	Learning how to express my feelings
12-60*	Existential factors	38	Learning that I must take ultimate responsibility for the way I live my life, no matter how much guidance and support I get from others
4-18*	Interpersonal learning (input)	38	Other members honestly telling me what they think of me
9-43	Family reenactment	31	Being in a group was, in a sense, like being in a big family, only this time, a more accepting and understanding family
2-10	Group cohesiveness	25	Belonging to a group of people who understood and accepted me
5-24	Interpersonal learning (output)	25	The group's giving me an opportunity to learn to approach others
3-12	Universality	25	Seeing I was just as well off as others
1-5	Altruism	25	Helping others and being important in their lives

*Items that were also chosen by adults for these categories.

together with warm support, empowered the group to be more trusting and less threatened and to work in an atmosphere in which sharing and risk taking were the norms for group interaction. By being less intrusive and directing, we shifted to more of a consulting role, although we continued to provide information clearly, and at times to reframe some of the problems presented. This was necessary for better understanding by us as well as the group members.

Other factors contributing to the group's success included setting a

Table 4
Items Less Helpful and Least Helpful to Adolescents

Item	Category	Percentage	Item Statement
10-49	Insight	60	Learning that I react to some people with feelings that somehow belong to earlier periods of my life
7-33	Catharsis	40	Expressing negative and/or positive feelings toward the group leader
8-40*	Identification	33	Finding someone in the group I could pattern myself after
4-20	Interpersonal learning (input)	27	Learning that sometimes I confuse people by not saying what I really think
6-28*	Guidance	27	Group members telling me what to do
8-36*	Identification	27	Trying to be like someone in the group who was better adjusted than I
10-50	Insight	27	Learning that how I feel and behave today is related to my childhood and development
12-59	Existential	27	Recognizing that, no matter how close I get to other people, I must still face life alone

*Items that were also chosen by adults for these categories.

policy requiring therapists to stay with the group for a minimum of six months to one year, and never having both therapists leave the group at the same time; regulating the turnover among group members, thereby allowing for more continuity and stability and fewer regressions; obtaining data from those members leaving the group to ensure maintaining relevant themes; and screening adolecents in the unit, resulting in a more sophisticated group capable of doing tough therapeutic work.

The clinical counselors and administrative staff in the adolescent unit played an important role in allowing our group to function effectively. When the unit was operating optimally, both on a clinical and administrative level, the adolescents could focus on important themes instead of devoting group time to dealing with environmental problems in the unit or other parts of the hospital. It also helped that the unit's clinical and administrative staff endorsed our group efforts with the adolescents.

AUTHORITY ISSUES REVISITED

One of the important themes raised in group was an issue that had been attempted at earlier stages but had not been handled very successfully. Several group members were exploring how they had historically responded to authority figures in their lives, including ward staff, teachers, and parents.

Many of the adolescents recounted how they used defiance, ignoring, and passive-aggressive maneuvers to manage their anxiety about dealing with significant adults. Group members sometimes laughed and commented on how stupidly they had behaved in the past. Others did not feel sufficiently distanced from their old behaviors to laugh at their immaturity.

We supported their capacity to own their old techniques in dealing with authority figures. We once commented that their authority struggles could be seen as interpersonal power issues, and from their reports, neither they nor the adults involved in the conflicts had been very competent.

This type of observation from us piqued many of the members' interest and served as a catalyst for subsequent discussions. Some group members took the position that most of their troubles in interpersonal situations were because of "lousy adults," while others felt that the difficulties with adults were essentially their own fault.

We responded to those extreme positions by stating that any interpersonal situation is the product of two people, injecting the notion that neither blaming others all the time nor feeling shameful about personal inadequacies leads to real learning or competency. We also pointed out that most people, including the adults in their lives, were doing the best they could in their interactions, even though the results were sometimes painful and unjust, and often ineffective and nonproductive.

This somewhat compassionate view created tension in the group, accompanied by relief among members who were developing the capacity to be more flexible in their basic attitudes about interpersonal relationships. But this confrontation and reframing of certain aspects of the struggles inherent in interpersonal relationships could not have been accomplished during the less cohesive era in group.

The general theme of dealing with authority figures led to discussions of situations operating in the adolescents' lives. One boy, Rich, reported that his mother had stuck with him through all his problems with school and drugs, but that his father had been in and out of this life over the last several years. Rich clearly had a strong sense of loyalty to his mother and strong feelings of hostility and alienation concerning his father.

In numerous prior group sessions, Rich had reported that there were "good" female clinical counselors and "bad" male clinical counselors in the adolescent unit. During stressful times in the group, Rich would see the female co-therapist as virtuous and the male co-therapist as less than noble. A perceptive female group member made an astute observation to Rich by saying, "Every time you get upset, you start blaming one of the guys and protecting one of the girls on the ward."

In an earlier group session, this interpretation would almost certainly have been ignored or perhaps rejected as nonsense, but at this stage it was received by all of us. We waited to see if any of the other members would comment on her interpretation, and soon a boy did. "She's right, you do do that." We asked Rich, "What do you think about what they are saying?" His response was, "I don't know, maybe."

The female co-therapist at this point began to describe how Rich had learned to survive in his family by protecting his mother and being angry at his father, and suggested that this may have happened over and over again when he was in a stressful situation in which he had to defend himself.

We both then explained that this process has a name—*splitting*—and began to explore whether the splitting phenomenon was operating for other group members. Many of them admitted they too had used this process at times of stress in their lives. Having a label put on the process of splitting, and learning that it was operating in other group members' lives was very helpful for both Rich and the others, which was reflected in deeper levels of sharing and insightful comments.

COMPETENCY OF PARENTS AND CAREGIVERS

Some of the other group themes developed at this time centered around dealing with parents or stepparents who had been physically and sexually abusive, themes that had not been produced earlier in our group in any meaningful way. There had been subtle hints that physical and sexual abuse had occurred, but those issues usually were briefly disclosed during the acting out or regressed period of the group, often in an attempt to justify feelings of anger toward adults or to evoke sympathy about their victimization by adults.

Tied to these themes were issues involving psychological neglect and abuse by disturbed parents, usually alcoholic or drug-abusing parents or both. Now, our adolescents were able to deal with such themes. Their courage and sensitivity in handling these issues were a powerful source of inspiration for us.

In one series of group sessions, every female in the group talked about enduring actual or threatened sexual abuse by a father, a stepfather, or an adult male relative. Once the first girl started talking about sexual abuse, a norm was established and the group became a safe place to talk about sexual abuse.

As the disclosures began to be made, the group focused on simply listening to the disclosures and not on giving advice or asking for clarification. Each adolescent appeared to want to tell her story about this painful part of her development but not have it analyzed. On a few occasions, one girl would offer emotional support to encourage a troubled member to tell her whole story about what had happened.

Although it is difficult to draw conclusions about the material produced in this area, some generalizations can be made. All the adolescents felt confused about why they had been sexually abused, wanting to know, "Why did it happen to me?" There was great deal of questioning about the role each girl had played in the sexual abuse, and a concern about responsibility for its happening.

An anger toward mothers or other women for failing to protect them surfaced. In some instances, there was despair that mothers had not helped them when they disclosed their dilemma. Some girls even suspected that their mothers had actually colluded in the sexual abuse. This information provided a great deal of material for us to process. The boys in the group seemed immobilized at times by this sexual content. Some seemed outraged and offered solutions such as running away or killing the abusers.

The group began to process this material with a sensitive recognition that each person's struggle with sexual abuse was a unique piece of business. We noted this observation, telling them that each girl had done something very special by sharing her experience. Now each was a resource person for the others.

At this point, our therapeutic explorations centered around the meaning of their confusion over their sexual abuse. One girl said, "I used to pretend it didn't happen and that it was a bad dream, because I was so disgusted." Another said, "I thought it was something special between me and my dad, but even I sort of knew something was wrong." Someone else said, "I didn't do anything about it until I was older, and I wonder why I didn't." We were very supportive and commended them for bringing this material up, reinforcing the notion that it was a very confusing part of their identities.

The group seemed to move gently and sensitively in subsequent sessions to how each female assessed the impact of the sexual abuse and how she felt about herself and her relationship with members of the opposite sex. They all felt the abuse had a negative impact on their feelings about themselves and was currently, or probably would be, detrimental to their relationships with members of the opposite sex.

A secondary theme to surface concerned adults and caregivers in general. They began to own a painful reality that they hadn't been parented very well in a broad range of areas and feared that they might turn out to be just like their parents. We stressed that although they might be somewhat like their parents when they grew up, it was an unrealistic and pessimistic view that they would simply be replicas of their parents.

This area proved to be extremely painful, and many of the adolescents cried about how they had wished for more loving parents and how frightening it was growing up without the things they had needed from their parents. We reflected that their observations were very accurate and very painful, that they had shown enormous psychological strength in talking about these painful things and great courage in realizing what faced them in growing up.

We emphasized that other teenagers who had not had the same degree of trouble in their families and in school felt some of the same fears about growing up and being able to take care of themselves in the world. This input puzzled many of the group members, revealing their belief that their fears and pain were related only to the abuse or neglect by their parents. This discussion, particularly of the notion that fear and pain are a part of mastering the normal problems of adolescence, appeared to be a source of encouragement to several group members. We were essentially telling them that they had some problems to work through in order to free themselves to work on the normal issues that are a part of everyone's adolescence.

PARTICIPATION

Each group member now seemed highly motivated to get as much from group as possible. They commented on group themes and indicated transition points, asking if the group was finished with a certain topic and could start on something else. "We really did well dealing with the sex stuff," was a typical comment.

These observations indicated to us that there was enough safety and freedom in the group not only to bring up sensitive topics, but also to interpret and evaluate the group process. Although the group as a whole was functioning exceptionally well, there was also a competitive element among members regarding individual consultations with the co-therapists and other group members in areas that would contribute to their personal competency.

PERSONAL POWER

Virtually all members disclosed problems about which they wanted feedback from the group. Tied to earlier comments by the co-therapists, this information reinforced the idea that there are ways of interacting in relationships that lead to feelings of power and ways that lead to feelings of powerlessness, and that much of adolescence consists of developing ways to be interpersonally powerful in a healthy fashion. This feedback seemed to give the group members permission to bring up very important issues about their feelings of powerlessness in interpersonal relationships.

One seventeen-year-old, Mike, presented a very complex issue to the group regarding personal power. He disclosed that one part of him would like to bring what he had learned back to his family to try to help his parents deal with their alcoholism and depression once he left the hospital; another part of him wanted to forget what had happened and just get on with his life, making his own way in the world. This problem generated strong feelings among all the group members, because it was something each one faced to varying degrees.

We listened to the group competently process this dilemma. In their feedback,they indicated that he was being overly dependent and attached to his parents and needed to become more independent to go on with his life. Other members said that if he got involved with trying to help his parents, it would pull him down and he would find himself back in the hospital with more problems than before.

We asked them to consider whether Mike could do something about both aspects of his conflict. The ensuing discussion focused on having his parents or his whole family go into therapy, reinforcing the idea that he was not responsible for parenting his parents. There was a real danger that if he tried to be a ''therapist'' to his parents, he ran a risk of having his difficulties recur.

The group supported Mike's desire to help his parents and his forgiveness of them for being poor role models and for parenting him ineffectively. This input moved the group to a realization of how strongly we are attached to our parents and how we feel a fervent sense of loyalty to them even if they have not been ''ideal'' parents. Mike chose not to come up with a resolution to the conflict, but thanked the group members for their suggestions. Agreeing that the problem was complex, all the group members expressed confidence that he had made a good beginning in dealing with it.

As each member talked about his or her specific problems, usually dealing with parents, siblings, or other significant family members, it became clear that they were feeling greater personal power to deal with the problems in their lives. Their openness in asking for and listening to feedback gave us the impression that many of our group members were developing healthy personal power in terms of authority and self-sufficiency.

RULES AND FRIENDSHIP

One of the most amazing discoveries at this point was that many of our adolescents were experiencing genuine peer friendships for the first time and were very excited about this event, commenting that they had never felt as close, connected, or trusting of other people as they had become toward the group members. They raised the interesting issue of whether this closeness was tied only to their experiences in group and whether they would return to their old kinds of peer relationships afterward.

Some felt that the friendships they had made in group would continue. Others stated how much they valued the honest feedback they had received as well as the opportunity to give feedback to others. One member revealed how loyal he felt to all the others and how special it was to have this group of friends. He confessed that he had never had friends prior to his hospitalization and group experience. The consensus was that most of the members saw themselves becoming more dependent on each other than on their parents or other adults in their lives.

We commented on their initial question about the role their hospitalization and group work played in their development of friendships. One member directly asked us if the friendships we observed in other groups continued after a member left the hospital. We were candid in revealing that although some former members had stopped by and indicated that certain friendships had continued after hospitalization, others had not. It was evident that some of the adolescents wre wishing the close bond of friendship developed in the group would continue; others realized that it would not be possible.

We asked the group members how the friendships they now experienced differed from those they had participated in before being in the group. For many, previous peer relationships centered around using drugs and, compared with current friendships, were not seen as true peer relationships. A positive feature of their current friendships was a feeling of mutual interest, acceptance, and respect totally absent in previous peer relationships.

Group members noted that true friends need to have the option of giving a wide range of feedback and the choice of rejecting such feedback without threatening the friendship. Finally, they indicated that a true friend must never try to take over your problems.

Being inpatients allowed males and females to have friendships that were not romantic or sexual in nature. Some of them even felt angry when group members in the ward became sexually involved with each other. An implicit rule for many of them was that friendships in the hospital should never turn into sexual partnerships. The adolescents saw sexual relationships among their peers as an activity that would upset the unit and cause problems among the ward members.

Sexual activity was seen as something that ward members could participate in on weekend passes or trial visits home. In a way, they viewed the group and the unit as a quasi family, and in that context they wanted to be protected from their sexual urges or romantic inclinations.

CLOSENESS AND INTIMACY

The discussion of friendship had a value in and of itself, but as we had come to learn, one theme usually was significant in preparing the group to talk about other topics. Now the group moved into issues of loving relationships and their fear about feeling too close or intimate with each other. Many of the girls recalled how scary the forced intimacy of sexual abuse had been. They speculated that after being abused it was going to be very difficult to feel close to another person.

Supporting their concern, we reflected that their early experiences would certainly play a role in future relationships. The female co-therapist commented that in some ways, those group members who had been sexually abused had a clearer picture of what they did not want in terms of closeness and intimacy. This comment elicited the angry response, "But what a price to pay!" Again and again, the victimization aspect of sexual abuse was a terribly powerful negative force to be dealt with by the group.

Some members began to speculate about how a person could be open, loving, and trusting in relationships and at the same time be protected from being hurt. This question had been raised in adult groups, but this was the first time we encountered it among our adolescents.

One group member interjected that there was no answer to that question. Another said it was stupid to go around being open and trusting with other people because you would be asking to get hurt. Still another said that you could be somewhat open and loving, but also cautious and watchful of your relationships.

We confided that for us, some relationships had become very special, while others—even those we worked at diligently—had ended, often quite painfully. We revealed that our special relationships had been a source of courage to continue to be optimistic about some future relationships becoming special ones.

At this point we felt very much in synchronization with the group members, more like consultants than directing therapists. It also seemed we had taken on more of the role of group member, and leadership was shared rather than carried on in a formal way by the therapists. Moreover, the group had matured to a level similar to that of growth groups, or groups in which one goal is to incorporate leaders as group members.

We felt highly trusted by the group members and felt as if we had known each adolescent longer than his or her actual time with us. There was a level of comfort in the group, with active listening and spontaneous feedback, that had not been experienced at earlier stages, and a sense that we cherished each other and could learn a great deal from each other.

We were advocates of their healthy, competent functioning, and they were advocates of the development of our skill in adolescent group therapy and our psychological well-being. There was a sense of reciprocal, authentic are being given.

TENDERNESS AND HUMOR

In the earlier stages of group development, when the group functioning was more primitive, we seldom saw any tenderness or humor expressed by group members. The situation now was quite different. We had seen some elements of compassion expressed in prior groups when a member was leaving, but now we observed genuine tenderness, mixed at times with emotional support and confrontation, displayed in discussions of issues other than a member's departure.

In one session, a group member, Steven, indicated early in the session that he wanted to discuss something very personal. He received the usual support and encouragement from the group and proceeded to announce, "I'm a homosexual." He discussed in detail how he had felt different throughout his life, and how he was strongly attracted to members of the same sex.

The girls responded with statements such as, "I hear what you're saying and it doesn't make any difference to me that you're a homosexual," and "I'm glad you told us because I imagine that's a hard thing to carry around without telling someone." Most of the boys echoed the girls' remarks. One said, "I'm not concerned about you being a homosexual; it doesn't make any difference because you're my friend."

Steven began to cry, and the group responded to this show of emotion with a few minutes of compassionate silence. Each adolescent began to give very tender verbal support. One said, "Let it go. Cry it out." Another said, "I'm with you all the way with this." This process was perhaps one of the most touching pieces of group business we had experienced.

Several weeks later, Julie, a girl who had a history of sexual abuse and promiscuous sexual activity, announced at the start of the session that someone had tried to proposition her just before group. We immediately called hospital security so that she could describe the man and the vehicle he was driving.

During the meeting we all listened to Julie's account of the incident.

She also talked about the sexual abuse she had endured at home from an uncle. At the end of the group she was interviewed by hospital security.

In the following session the incident was brought up again by the group. Julie was asked how she felt about being propositioned at the hospital and about the sexual abuse at home. This processing began without any criticism and with the members' obvious intention to be helpful to her. She reopened the issue of sexual abuse, recounting how angry she was that her mother had not helped her when she told her about the problem. She disclosed that "guys" always made sexual advances to her and that she did not know the reason for their behavior.

The other girls confronted her with their impression that she was very seductive in the way she dressed, and that she came on too strong. This observation was made compassionately and uncritically and was received well by Julie. Another group member said she was very concerned that Julie had been used sexually by her uncle and, in a way, continued to be used sexually by other males. Both the males and females said she was too good a person to continue being treated this way.

Julie cried after these statements were made and revealed that she was now thinking about how she could change her behavior with boys. Everyone suggested that she practice new ways of talking and dealing with males and get feedback on how she was coming across. The tenderness, confrontation, and problem solving all were very powerful interventions at this phase of the group's development.

Another example of the group's sensitivity involved a disturbed seventeen-year-old who was extremely anxious in group and often made inappropriate comments. Jean's association became very loose whenever the tension level increased.

In earlier group sessions such behavior would have been greeted by rejecting hostility or heavy criticism. In the present context it became clear that her loose associations played a significant role in protecting her from threatening situations. She related how once, at home, when her mother and father were arguing and were about to become involved in a physical confrontation, she started yelling, "The water on the stove is boiling over," which distracted her parents from hitting each other, and so did serve a protective purpose.

The group members seemed fascinated both by her symptom and by the powerful role it played in her life. When her loose association occurred in group, her fellow members asked her to identify what she feared was going to happen in group. Whenever she was less anxious, the group members, particularly the boys, commented that she was really "hanging in there." This patient seemed well aware of the group's efforts to deal with her symptom kindly, and she appreciated their endorsement and continuing involvement both in the group and in the ward.

SUMMARY AND CONCLUSIONS

In short, this phase was characterized by an increase of genuine acceptance and healthy functioning and a decrease of psychopathological functioning. We were also impressed that adolescents could be very powerful caregivers to each other when they had some understanding of the elements involved in their respective struggles.

Our group members were now demonstrating a powerful caring for each other, not orchestrated by us, which showed an amazing sensitivity and strength on their part. We were aware of increased social competence and an expansion of functional roles performed by each member.

Equally important was the breakdown of barriers between the therapists and group members and our acceptance and incorporation as group members, albeit older members who possessed valuable information.

The adolescents speculated about the quality of friendships among the clinical counselors in the unit, observing that some of the counselors did not seem to have friendships as close as the ones they had developed. They had occasionally witnessed the counselors' manipulation of and lack of caring for each other. They were also aware of those counselors who used drugs, particularly marijuana, and those who were depressed.

This focus on staff relationships shifted toward our relationship outside of the group. Some members asked us if we were as kind to each other outside the group as we were within. We responded that just as they had developed strong friendships, we too had become good friends working together in group and, because of the close bond developed around our group work, were indeed special friends to each other.

Friendship proved to be an important deficit area for the adolescents, helped by the group experience. Underlying issues of personal commitment and loyalty in relationships had been addressed. Their fidelity to one another and speculation on the fidelity of others were very important pieces of group business and critically important factors in making healthy adjustments outside of the hospital.

9

WHY CO-THERAPY?

It takes two to speak the truth—one to speak, and another to hear.
—Henry David Thoreau

We are fully committed by belief and experience to the co-therapy model for treating adolescents in group psychotherapy, and so this chapter examines the special issues pertaining to co-therapy. Our observations apply equally to co-therapy in all therapeutic groups, regardless of the age, sex, or diagnosis of group members.

Some authors have specified co-therapy for special populations, for example, borderlines (Greenblum and Pinney, 1982), narcissists, and schizophrenics (Rutan and Alonso, 1980), noting the advantages of co-therapy in dealing with the complexities, transferences, countertransferences, and the like found in most groups.

Our position is that groups that are properly conducted by co-therapists can benefit all patients, with the exception of mute individuals or hospitalized chronics at the extreme in lower energy. Research shows gains with those patients are so limited and changes so slight that group work is impractical, despite the concerted efforts of the co-therapists.

BENEFITS OF CO-THERAPY

Bernard, Drob, and Lifshutz (1987) have effectively summarized the value of co-therapy in groups. Based on their eight points, we have developed a series of considerations regarding the efficacy of co-therapy.

First, co-therapy increases effective monitoring. When one therapist becomes entrapped, confused, or uncertain, the co-therapist may supply a clarification or a different perspective or simply "bail out" the partner.

This is more common than might be supposed. Even under the most ideal conditions, a therapist cannot attend to all the group's comments and actions. Studies of attending, monitoring, or observing group behavior have placed the norm at about 70 percent awareness of what is occurring.

Even if the therapist is highly motivated, images and memories will be triggered by group members' responses, and in those moments the words or actions of the speaker may be missed. The co-therapist's presence greatly reduces the possibility that some important response will be completely lost.

When reviewing video or audio tapes, we have often been surprised to discover material that had escaped our awareness during the actual session. We have a policy of recording sessions even when both co-therapists are highly experienced. We also process these materials regularly. These postsession analyses can provide important information about the session as well as reveal issues to be dealt with in future meetings.

A second benefit of co-therapy is that the background and experiences of the co-therapists can enrich and expand the knowledge base beyond that possible for a single therapist. When possible, co-therapy should be conducted by a male and a female. This not only creates a family model for the group, but it gives the group the resources of both sexual developmental and social systems that are part of child rearing in our culture.

This is not to suggest any role stereotyping. Effective co-therapists rarely could be identified as heavily committed to a sex role to the exclusion of a more androgynous, rich awareness of opposite-sex–role behavior. A therapist who cannot function androgynously, both strongly and tenderly, both feeling and action oriented, would perform with a serious deficit in most adolescent therapy groups. A soft, passive, self-effacing female therapist would do poorly in most groups as would a distant, autocratic, paternal male therapist.

While it is rare that a perfect balance can be maintained on these dimensions, effective co-therapists are self-aware and able to attain workable levels of appropriate role behaviors that meet the needs of group members.

A third benefit is found in the co-therapists' modeling , which is critically important in the adolescent group. Coming from backgrounds of abuse, inadequate parenting, and attachment deficits, and often having experienced only defective models, the group members observe, study, and often incorporate the co-therapists' interactions into their own behavior patterns.

The interactions between the co-therapists, therefore, must be direct, open, supportive, mature, and communicative. The subtly snide, the cute, or the condescending have no place in the interactions between co-therapists. Mature communication can and does have both playful and humorous aspects that are important to the group session.

When differences occur between co-therapists, they should always be processed after the group session. It is possible to express different points of view in an open, nondefensive way that can model for the group the fact that in a mature relationship all parties do not have to share the same view.

Although the male therapist has often supported the female therapist's view, he usually adds that ''growing up male'' has given him a different perspective. The message received by the group is that dialogue is important, individual views are respected, and each person is unique.

A fourth benefit of co-therapy is that it provides a continuity of care. If one therapist is absent because of illness or vacation, continuity in the group is maintained by the other therapist. In a co-therapist's absence, the group invariably deals with feelings of rejection (in the case of a vacation) or concern (in the case of illness). There is a similar but less intense response when a group member is absent.

When a trainee's time with the group ends, there is a reaction that follows the well-described steps of the grief process: disbelief, depression, anger, and recovery. This is magnified if the trainee has been a true co-therapist and has functioned effectively in the group. In all these instances, the senior co-therapist is challenged to be omnipotent and to fix the situation. When that does not happen, the group may react against the therapist with hostility and depression.

Although it has not happened with us, many groups have experienced the death of a co-therapist. There are accounts in the literature of the resources and reactions of groups, with recommendations on processing and working through their feelings.

SOURCES OF DIFFICULTY

From our experience, co-therapists who model sharing, disclosing, noncontrolling, healthy relationships have provided major benefits for the group and each other. If the co-therapists are not successfully matched, however, the group will not reach its potential under this treatment approach. We agree with the findings of Bernard et al. (1987) that similar and compatible therapy styles are an absolute requirement for the successful group. They found that therapists who involve themselves in similar self-disclosure and levels of awareness in their client contacts were most likely to be compatible as co-therapists.

Problems in the co-therapy relationship can be traced directly to a series of functional differences, many of which have been detailed by researchers, beginning as early as 1952 (Lundin and Aranov) and continuing, in limited number, to the present. We have found that most difficulties arise from therapists' problems relating to control, dominance, blind spots, unresolved adolescent conflicts, and the inability to give and receive feedback.

Problems involving control are based on a therapist's need or desire to fix, improve, or change the adolescents. This need implies that the therapist knows what each group member's appropriate role and behavior are and works toward those goals. If both therapists share this position, a parenting model develops, which, however well-intentioned, can only perform those kinds of interventions. In its worst form it can be a folie à deux of the therapists, whereby conflicting views can create a dysfunctional family model played out by the co-therapists.

Dominance is a second problem area. Experienced therapists are often tempted to share with less-experienced colleagues—without being asked—the wealth of their knowledge. This may occur during any phase of group activity, from the playing phase to the selection of participants, from the group sessions to the debriefing sessions that follow. In its most pathological form, dominance involves one therapist overruling the other with rules, recommendations, or control messages in the group session.

It is certainly appropriate for co-therapists to express differing views on issues, but they should do so in the spirit of inquiry and with the goal of conveying to group members that other views are respected and accepted and, in a functional relationship, provide a depth and richness that can only occur when territorial concerns are set aside and all persons involved engage in a problem-solving approach.

Blind spots present a third problem in co-therapy. Most therapists have blind spots, often because of limited experience or lack of exposure to some significant cultural differences, or because of racial, ethnic, or sex differences that prevent them from fully comprehending an issue or problem described by a group member.

Effective therapy involves much new learning for the co-therapists. An admission of ignorance or awareness of a belief, practice, or language usage may permit group members to become the teachers and to educate the therapist. The message to the group is one of respect for the information, a willingness to listen, and an opportunity to try out new sets of behaviors, all of which are rarely granted in the home environment.

Unresolved adolescent conflicts can be one of the most destructive or corrosive elements in the co-therapy relationship. Problems involving control, dominance, and blind spots often emerge when the group touches too closely on issues that were unresolved in the therapist's youth. Most often their unresolved issues involve conflicts or attitudes with one or both parents, a need to rebel against parental authority, or an attempt to savor missing experiences or recapture experiences gone too soon.

Adolescent concerns such as dependency-independency, sexuality (both heterosexual and homosexual), guilt, religiosity, models for achievement or nonachievement, and peer and family attachment problems may, for some therapists, be unresolved, repressed, and covered by a layer of new knowledge.

If these issues have not had satisfactory and successful resolution, the individual is at risk as an adolescent therapist and particularly as a co-therapist. There is no place in adolescent group psychotherapy for one or both therapists to work through their adolescent conflicts in the presence of adolescent group members.

Many therapists avoid undertaking therapy with adolescents for these very reasons. However, training for residents and interns often requires rotation to the adolescent service, and captives in this setting may have great difficulty functioning effectively in groups. They may take on a variety of roles: parent, administrator, guidance counselor, adviser, pal, or even ego ideal. The manifestations can be oppositional behavior toward the co-therapist, joining with the adolescent group members either collectively or by pairing.

Such problems are difficult to resolve, although many can be dealt with in the debriefing period. If that proves ineffective, a series of observations by a third therapist can provide constructive feedback to the co-therapist and, it is hoped, modify the undesired behaviors. Failing in these efforts, reassignment appears to be the remaining solution.

There will, of course, be reminiscences that may require discussion and working through during the posttherapy debriefing session, but these should be minimal: asking a co-therapist where certain feelings may have arisen, if it appears that the material can be processed easily and successfully. Should painful and traumatic repressed material be uncovered, it should be explored to determine whether the co-therapists can work through it together, or whether a third person should be sought to provide a brief intervention. In our experience, it has rarely been necessary to seek additional resources. The solid relationship and trust between the co-therapists were enough to resolve the issue.

A sexual relationship between the co-therapists, on the other hand, could have a negative impact on the group. Effective co-therapy involves caring, sharing, trust, openness, and self-disclosure between the co-therapists, all ingredients of a good relationship.

Sex could be a natural consequence of such a relationship, but in our view this would distort the relationship. It might be disclosed to the group through subtle behaviors, with a negative effect, especially if it involved an extramarital affair.

If co-therapists appear to have a special relationship with each other, it can alienate them from other staff. Further, if such a relationship were to encounter difficulty, the strained interactions between the co-therapists would be observed by the group and result in discomfort and even a role reversal, with the patients seeking to heal the co-therapists.

Even under the best of circumstances, the co-therapy relationship may be questioned by husbands, wives, or significant others. Time spent with a co-therapist, expressed admiration for the colleague, and exclusion of significant others because of a need for confidentiality all serve to create doubt and alienation. Bowers and Gauron (1981) strongly suggest orientation and demythization for spouses and significant others.

Finally, feedback presents a potential problem for the co-therapists. There is no question that providing feedback to professional equals is one of the most difficult things a therapist can engage in; only receiving feedback can be more difficult. Improperly given feedback can take the form of an attack or can be perceived that way. In our experience, feedback works best if the person who is to receive it is first given the opportunity to provide his or her perceptions of what took place and of his or her performance.

Most therapists, both those in training and professionals, are keenly perceptive and, if anything, overly self-critical. Feedback should be an adding to, a shaping, and an expansion of their statements and ideas, rather than the observations of an omniscient co-therapist. If the perceptions of the co-therapist are off target or seem to be projections or misconceptions, feedback focuses on correcting, seeking the source of the misconceptions, or clarification of expressed views. As this exploration evolves, a dialogue ensues in which a fuller understanding is achieved.

If differences and resistance appear at this point, we would suggest a review of the video or audio tape so the co-therapists can evaluate together what actually took place. What typically emerges is recognition on the part of the recipient of the negative feedback and, often, a softening on the part of the giver of the feedback, especially if there are positive behaviors noted about which positive feedback can be given.

The model for co-therapists does not emerge automatically. With many of our co-therapists and trainees, high levels of communication and effectiveness were achieved. In other instances, pairings were limited by issues of authority, problems of communication, or lack of role flexibility.

In our experiences, one trainee continually fell asleep during group sessions as a defense against anxiety. Another tried to compete with the co-therapist for group approval. A third, extremely anxious about his professional role, became counterdefensive and withdrew from active participation. In each instance an impasse was reached that could only be resolved through termination of the trainee.

This was not handled in an arbitrary or unilateral manner. Through discussions, recommendations, and finally the intervention of a third observer, we sought to provide feedback and restructuring for the co-therapist expressing difficulties. For most trainees, these interventions succeeded; for the three examples described, the ability to change was lacking.

Each session of psychotherapy should have a postsession evaluation between the co-therapists for processing or debriefing. The content typically is wide-ranging and inclusive, and follows the topics outlined by Corder, Russell, and Koehne (1984-85): curative factors needing emphasis; group techniques to be considered, such as role playing and relaxation techniques; group members requiring extra assistance or focus; problems in the co-therapists' interactions that need to be watched; and administrative issues to be handled, such as forms, reports, and testing. To that list we would add a discussion of personal feelings, hunches, and speculations, and an attempt to capture a global sense of the group and its evolution.

Because mutual feedback is the essential ingredient of the posttherapy session, it is imperative that it occur immediately following the group rather than days later or before the next group meeting. In the cases mentioned in which co-therapy did not succeed, feedback was usually met with defensive or evasive responses and a failure to confront or deal with issues. Instead of attempting to explore issues openly and explain observed behavior, the behavior was denied, and in some instances, the co-therapist was blamed.

Each of these cases involved therapists in training, and the lines of responsibility rested first with the senior therapist, although trainees were encouraged to function as co-equals. They were expected to involve themselves fully in the group upon taking the co-therapist's role. For some, a period of group observation, discussion, and study preceded active participation in the group.

Every attempt was made to reduce the hierarchical ranking of the co-therapists, but as many writers point out, this is not a simple thing to do. Bernard, Babineau, and Schwartz (1980) discuss the problems and strengths of co-therapy as a training model. Bowers and Gauron (1981) describe hazards for patients as well as co-therapists. Principally, they feel that patients suffer when the co-therapy relationship supersedes the importance of the treatment of patients, when co-therapists share to the exclusion of patients, and when defective modeling occurs. Shainess (1977) indicates that patients in a group are often childlike and carefully observe what the therapists do in order to judge, identify, copy, and decide whether or not they are trustworthy.

DEMOGRAPHIC FACTORS

A number of demographic factors can affect the co-therapy relationship, including sex, age, race, ethnicity, experience, position, and physical characteristics. These factors are presented from the analytic perspective in the work of Davis and Lohr (1971). Our perceptions, which are both behavioral and dynamic, are in agreement with their observations.

Ideally, co-therapists should represent both sexes, although we have conducted groups with co-therapists of the same sex. Many issues are immediately facilitated by having a male and a female present, although in practice, the role behavior is more significant than is the sex of a therapist.

Effective psychotherapists, male and female, have role flexibility and can move easily from traditionally male sex roles to traditionally female sex roles. Although we are aware of no studies that have reported this finding, it is our belief that effective therapists would score as androgynous on measures relating to sex roles.

If both co-therapists are of the same sex, it is important that they use behaviors beyond those viewed as stereotypical of that sex. Professionals who appear to have deeply ingrained sex-typing seem to find group psychotherapy less appealing than other therapeutic approaches offering greater control.

The co-therapists' ages present a variety of issues to group members and to the co-therapists as well. For group members, a youthful therapist may represent the potential of a slightly older peer, a love object, or someone to manipulate because of suspected inexperience. Conversely, older therapists with gray hair or other signs of aging may be stereotyped as authority figures, parents, members of the establishment, or generally representative of an oppressive part of the adolescent's experience.

It has been our experience that unless the therapist has unresolved concerns relating to age or to his or her therapeutic role, these issues can be dealt with in the group by the openness, caring, and therapeutic efforts of the therapists.

Our experience has included working with co-therapists of different races and ethnic origins. Because we practice in the South, we have tried to be especially sensitive to these issues. Despite initial questions raised by group members regarding race and ethnicity, the openness of the co-therapists helped the group members relate to the therapists as individuals rather than locking them into stereotypical roles or sets of attitudes.

Had these been issues between the co-therapists, group members would have sensed their questions or discomfort and reflected or mirrored that in their behavior. A therapist must understand the values and views of his or her co-therapist and be aware of and sensitive to ethnic and racial views, behavior, and history. If the racial or ethnic awareness of the co-therapists is limited with regard to some group members, the situation affords an excellent opportunity for the patient to become the teacher by broadening the awareness of the therapists.

The amount of experience each therapist has can also affect the relationship between co-therapists. Most often, the less-experienced therapist defers to the more experienced one. The younger co-therapist may also exhibit adolescent rebellion based on unresolved issues with parents or authority figures. Fortunately, this rarely extends beyond the trainee status, although it is quite common for group members to infer and assign higher responsibility, not necessarily status, to the older co-therapist.

We have found that this can be handled simply and easily by redirecting material that comes from group members acting on a stereotype. For example, a question implying the greater responsibility of the older co-therapist can be redirected to the younger co-therapist. Conversely, an issue on which the younger co-therapist is felt to understand an adolescent's position can be redirected to the older co-therapist. (Questions implying stereotypical sex-role perceptions can be redirected in a similar manner.)

We would not agree that ''good co-therapists are born, not made,'' nor have we found that any single program can provide assurance that its graduates have a greater therapeutic potential or skill in group psychotherapy. Indeed, those programs that foster autocratic or authoritative attitudes in their trainees lay groundwork that can only be overcome with extreme difficulty, if at all.

We have worked with co-therapists from nursing, social work, psychology, psychiatry, and even paraprofessional training, and have found sensitive and highly competent persons in each area. Conversely, we have found persons from each area who were inexperienced and insensitive to the group process. There is a potential for resentment, mistrust, and other difficulties based on professional role differences because of differential status accorded by other staff, the community, and, on rare occasions, by group members. These issues must be resolved as they arise to prevent damage to the group.

Should such a problem occur, however, it can appear to be a re-enactment of family traumas experienced by group members. For example, a psychiatrist conducting a group with a colleague who is not a psychiatrist might be a ''father [or mother] knows best'' model, especially if the psychiatrist believes that others cannot possess his or her skill in a group.

As with age and race or ethnicity, physical appearance presents a direct and meaningful stimulus to the adolescent group, whether due to physical characteristics, attire, or a deformity or disability a co-therapist might have. Often this is a source of concern or curiosity for the group and even for a co-therapist.

Where this appears to be an issue, noted by expressive, nonverbal, or other means, it is essential to the group's growth and development that these feelings be explored. For example, a handicapped co-therapist might be engaged in a dialogue by the other co-therapist in which his or her feelings, attitudes, and special problems are shared with the group. This model of sharing and openness has the dramatic effect of breaking through group resistances and reluctance to think about and share feelings.

With regard to personal attributes and grooming, all therapists must be keenly aware of the actual and potential impact extremes in dress style may have on group members, moving as they do from being relatively ambiguous stimuli to all the stereotypes that may accrue to certain styles of dress or grooming.

For example, a male therapist's shoulder-length hair and casual dress may be statements of his independence from professional supervisors and authority figures. These characteristics and his statements may communicate this to group members, further adding to their already alienated attitudes. He can retain his preferred hair length and dress, but he should take pains to see that they do not represent an attempt to form alliances with the adolescent group members, and he must, above all, remain a fully professional therapist.

Each aspect of personal appearance has its implications. To prevent any miscommunication, group members, co-therapists, and others having an impact on the group should carefully explore both within themselves and through feedback the impact of their personal appearance.

In our view, one of the major differences between beginning and experienced co-therapists (and successful and unsuccessful ones, as well) is the degree of self-monitoring that takes place. Beginning therapists frequently fail to observe significant statements and actions taking place in the group because their attention is focused intrnally, checking on *their own* feelings, *their own* actions, and *their own* behavior, rather than being focused on the group.

The response is not unlike that of their patients, whose initial responses in the group are egocentric and often narcissistic. Indeed, the major milestone in all psychotherapy is a movement from this self-attention to the inclusion of others in their concerns. But this response is not unique to co-therapists. High levels of self-monitoring and self-doubt occur in virtually every activity that may be subject to critical evaluation. Acting, sports, presentations, in their initial phases, have similar patterns.

This is not to suggest that for experienced therapists no self-monitoring takes place. It is minimal, however, and may simply be related to the desirability or timing of an intervention or to the appropriateness of certain requests for self-disclosure by the co-therapist. The major focus of both therapists should be the activity taking place in the group and a sensitivity to what is taking place with the co-therapist.

Ideally, both therapists should reach this level of group focus. They must play flexible and presumably androgynous roles for the group; they must be able, when appropriate, to self-disclose to the group; and they must always be open, self-disclosing, and sensitive to each other in the debriefing and processing period following the group. We see these as the critical factors in effective co-therapy.

We would also agree with a series of studies that stress the importance of similar theoretical orientation (McMahon and Links, 1984; Hellwig and Memmot, 1974; Paulson, Burroughs, and Gelb, 1976); the endorsing of the co-therapy pair in which the self-esteem of each therapist is fostered; a testing phase in which competencies and sharing are explored; and a role-clarification phase in which role and style differences emerge, boundaries are established, and equality of personal gratification is resolved (McMahon and Links).

As the issues are resolved, the co-therapists become a cohesive unit working effectively in concert with one another. This is not to suggest that problems do not arise; conflicts do occur and differences of opinion arise. But within this framework, it is possible to deal with all issues.

As with any successful relationship, the gratifications of co-therapy involve the co-therapists' awareness of each other's feelings, intentions, and observations; a sharing of goals; and the supplementing, enhancing, and improving of each other's ideas, with the additional bonus that each is a source of support for the other. This is the basis of a very important and special relationship.

PERSONALITY DYNAMICS

In addition to demographic factors, cognitions, affective displays, defense mechanisms, ego issues, and synchronicity affect the co-therapists' relationship. Each presents behaviors and issues to resolve, understand, and relate to. When the pieces fit together, the group is the beneficiary of a totally healthy, functioning, communicating model. This can only be achieved by sharing, self-exploration, and high levels of communication.

With regard to response style, the co-therapists must become comfortable with the content, frequency, and manner of presentation of each other's inputs and interventions. There is no place in adolescent group therapy for a dominating, omniscient therapist, or one who presents material in a parental or condescending style. Such issues should be resolved during training.

Aside from those extremes, there is a wide range of response styles that will require adjusting, understanding, and agreement on pace and timing. Thus it is possible to be quiet, reserved, ascendant, and expressive, as a preferred style, provided the therapist can shift to other modes as required in the sense in which Horney described the healthy individual's ability to move toward, away from, or against others as situationally appropriate.

Each co-therapist has, and uses, certain affect displays and defense mechanisms; each may be competitive under certain circumstances. These factors, however, should not play a significant role in interaction with group members. This should be understood well by one's co-therapist so an appropriate and defusing intervention can be made if the co-therapist becomes reactive in a nontherapeutic manner. In such situations, we have found that such interventions typically take on a humorous twist, involving comments such as, "Am I rambling again?" or "Am I sounding too nostalgic?"

Our concern is to minimize any defensive responses on the part of the co-therapy team. The message communicated to group members, as with other conflicts and misunderstandings, is one of a defective relationship, not unlike that which they have experienced in their family. We have indicated the importance of modeling; uncorrected defective interactions communicate an inappropriate message.

The goal of synchronous behavior on the part of the co-therapy team does allow for different views, however, but these differences are always respected, always heard, and always dealt with in a sympathetic and understanding manner. Group members observing differences discover the rich diversity and breadth of views, not the anger and hostility generated in families when differences of opinion arise or alternate views surface.

SUMMARY

In this chapter we have presented some of the necessary conditions for the successful co-therapy we feel is most desirable, if not a ncessity, for successful adolescent group psychotherapy.

The blending of two competent professionals into a functioning, cohesive unit sharing at many levels with one another and with their group requires a great deal of effort and the highest levels of communication. We have detailed both strengths and possible difficulties the team may encounter and have suggested methods for dealing with areas of potential conflict.

10

TRAINING AND SUPERVISION

> Training that brings about no change is as effective as a parachute that opens on the first bounce.
>
> —Anonymous

This chapter initially examines the work of Averill et al. (1973), who were involved in teaching and supervising group therapists at the Boys' Industrial School in Topeka, Kansas. Their work with male adolescents has a strong parallel to our adolescent group therapy program at the Hall Institute during the 1970s and early 1980s.

We also review some of the issues encountered with trainee therapists in our program and discuss the characteristics of effective and ineffective adolescent group therapists.

THE BOYS' INDUSTRIAL SCHOOL

Averill and colleagues point out that the novice adolescent group therapist usually has numerous preconceived ideas, apprehensions, and reservations prior to starting work as a therapist. Their orientation program for the beginning therapist included an introduction to the major literary contributions in the field of delinquency and psychotherapy (such as Aichorn and Winnicott), and participation in the Psychotherapists' Supervisory Group, which dealt with the male delinquents the new therapist would encounter in group therapy and the goals and expectations of the group psychotherapy treatment modality.

The therapeutic goals at the Boys' Industrial School were to help the boys (1) become more comfortable in their relationships with adults and peers; (2) recognize and identify the feelings and impulses aroused in their relationships with others; (3) learn that many of the fears, wishes, impulses, and thoughts they considered unique are common to many people; (4) become aware of the feelings, impulses, tensions, and anxieties that cause them to act up or act out; (5) develop the ability to tolerate feelings without acting until they can appropriately assess present reality; and (6) learn to express their feelings, wishes, fears, and hopes openly and directly in words to discover that more rewarding and gratifying relationships can take place.

The group therapy program played a major role in helping group members reach these goals. The average length of stay at the school was fourteen months for the adolescents and approximately one year for the therapist. Consequently, commitments to intensive, long-term treatment were seldom made.

All beginning therapists were given an outline of group psychotherapy as done at the school and encouraged to read it and discuss the issues in the Psychotherapists' Supervisory Group. The outline, consisting of theoretical assumptions, observations, and case examples, all helped the new therapists understand the boys, learn about the group process, and avoid common pitfalls.

Each group psychotherapist was given the following instructions and passed these principles on to the group members over a period of time:

1. The group is to talk and not act.
2. No more limits will be set than absolutely necessary for the safety of the boys.
3. Remarks of the psychotherapist are to be directed to the group rather than to individuals whenever possible.
4. The boys are free to talk about whatever is important to them.
5. All action, particularly of a negative or hostile nature, is to be commented upon by the therapist and an effort made to bring out its verbal equivalent.
6. Create a warm and accepting atmosphere in the group.
7. Do not allow the boys to scapegoat a member or project too much hostility outside the immediate situation. Invite the boys to direct hostility toward the psychotherapist.

The insights that it was hoped the boys would gain over a period of time were the following:

1. All behavior has meaning.

2. Much of the boys' behavior is self-defeating and compulsive in nature.
3. The boys act toward adults in authority in a stereotyped manner as though all adults are the same and all are bad.
4. The boys are angry at their parents but are afraid to express this because they need them too much.
5. The boys are dependent on other people, and this is possible without fear if they can distinguish adults from each other.
6. The boys are not as bad as they think they are, but they will never be as perfect as they wish to be.
7. Change and progress come from constructive effort.
8. The boys should become aware of and tolerate anxiety, sadness, and hopeless feelings without acting on them.

According to Averill et al. (1973), the role of the therapist in the group is one in which focus is on the interests and concerns of the members, not on the agendas of the therapist nor on the issues of the institution. It is also necessary that discussions are open and safe, taking place in a climate where self-understanding can occur and where new behaviors can be attempted by the adolescents with more adequate and appropriate methods for fulfilling their needs.

It is important that the therapist function as an adult and not join the counterdependency of group members in their interactions with authority. To share the group members' resentment of authority, to challenge with them the rules of the institution, effectively undermines and destroys the role of the therapist. It would no longer be possible for the therapist to be a transference object on whom "the boys can project their feelings, impulses, attitudes, hopes and fears." The therapist should remain at all times real and, according to the authors, "an adult and a staff member who represents society at large."

Averill and colleagues also addressed issues for the new therapist, which were addressed through the formation of a Psychotherapists' Supervisory Group—a personal growth and learning group for staff therapists in which they try to obtain greater understanding of the boys they treat, some understanding of their role and their responsibilities, experience with the group process, staff cohesiveness, and increased self-understanding. In many ways, this group is a parallel experience for staff therapists to that of the boys in the group they conduct.

METHODS USED IN TRAINING

We mentioned that we had a mandate to train mental health trainees to do adolescent group therapy. We used several methods to teach our particular model to the predoctoral clinical psychology interns and child psychiatry fellows involved in the adolescent inpatient service. Just as necessity had been the mother of invention in the evolution of our model of group therapy, necessity played a major role in the development of training strategies.

DIRECT OBSERVATION AND VIDEOTAPES

In the early stages of our training approach, we had trainees observe us in the group. Immediately after each group, we had a discussion with the trainees about what they saw and what we were attempting to do in the group. Occasionally we would videotape several sessions and review them with the trainees and adolescent group members. Examining the tapes with the trainees produced several benefits, including a much more orderly and focused discussion of various aspects of the group.

Having the option to reconsider one part of a difficult group problem gave the trainees valuable data that otherwise would not have been obtained in the regular discussion groups after each session. When we reviewed the videotapes with the adolescents, some of our patients became so embarrassed that they could not look at the tape; others claimed to be amazed both by how they looked and by the negative quality of their behavior.

Videotaping helped us to move through trying stages in the group, usually periods of high tension, acting out, or low energy. We elected not to have videotaping on a regular basis, however, because, while it served to help with immediate dilemmas, it was also a distraction in developing a group competent in verbal interaction.

The trainees watched us in sessions or on videotape as they prepared to join the group as co-therapists. Their entrance into the group was often made painful by the adolescents because of their "trainee status." The group members challenged their lack of experience as therapists and knew their tenure was limited to completion of their training.

Because of this situation, the trainee co-therapists would sometimes choose to be passive observers in the group, as opposed to taking a more active co-therapy role. The adolescents often focused their interaction on the staff co-therapist, either ignoring or defying any verbal inputs from the trainee. A few times group members referred to the group as being the staff member's group, in essence neutralizing the notion that the staff and trainee co-therapists were both leaders of the group.

In our supervisory sessions, we dealt with this issue fairly directly. Some trainees saw the situation as one in which the group actually belonged to the staff co-therapist; others were satisfied to play the role of observer co-therapist, knowing they would have the opportunity at a later date to lead a group on their own. A few of the trainees demanded a more equal status. They all confronted the same problem we had faced when we began the therapy program: acceptance as therapists by the adolescents.

We addressed the issue that our trainees were not operating as peer co-therapists, and the special problems this presented. Our recognition of this fact appeared to help the trainees with their feelings of awkwardness in their role as co-therapists in the group. We explained how the co-therapy relationship had been clinically productive and personally rewarding for us. We provided the trainees with data from the psychotherapy literature about the value of the co-therapy relationship in groups.

Our input was similar to the summary provided in an article by Bernard et al. (1987), giving the advantages inherent in the co-therapy arrangement. Among the benefits these authors point to are that it

1. Decreases anxiety when therapists are trainees (''shared burden'' hypothesis);
2. Enhances the perspective brought to bear about individuals, patients, and group process, and therefore the potential for understanding clinical data;
3. Provides a model of a healthy relationship, which can lead to a corrective emotional experience for patients whose parents interacted destructively (when co-therapists collaborate effectively);
4. Enhances limit-setting capacity with severely disturbed patients;
5. Provides in vivo support and peer supervision for therapists struggling with patients' psychopathology and with learning a new treatment modality;
6. Affords continuity of care when one therapist is away;
7. Compensates for individual therapist's limitations (when co-therapists complement each other);
8. Leads to perceived splits between the therapists (e.g., nurturing versus confronting), which can be examined to good therapeutic effect.

We also accentuated how critically important it was for both co-therapists to be active leaders in the group; a skewed distribution of status and power would have a detrimental effect on group process and context as the group went through various developmental phases. We emphasized what other authors have reported as the strengths of the balanced co-therapy relationship. From a clinical perspective, we told them how our relationship as co-therapists played a critical role in the evolution of our current group therapy model.

An important research study by Hurst, Stein, Korchin, and Soskin (1978) was presented to them, in which the authors explored how a therapist's or leader's style influences the development of cohesiveness in an adolescent personal growth group led by male and female co-leaders. The findings indicated that both therapists must separately exhibit effective leadership—for example, at least a medium to high amount of self-expressiveness and personal warmth—in order to facilitate cohesiveness in their group.

It does not appear that one leader can compensate for the other's lack or deficiency in one of these two areas. A high level of caring helps create a trusting, supportive atmosphere in which sharing and risk taking become less threatening. Self-expressiveness, namely the expression of feelings or the sharing of oneself with the group, implies that the group is a safe, trusting environment. When the leaders exhibit this behavior, they are making a statement of trust that they feel the group is safe. Giving our trainees clinical data about our experiences and information from the literature seemed to be helpful as they were learning to become adolescent group therapists.

As our group therapy model became more developed, we decided to try another approach in working with the trainee therapists. Instead of having one trainee paired with one of us, we let pairs of trainees lead the group while we observed their work This arrangement overcame some of the problems inherent in the staff–trainee co-therapist pairing but created another set of problems to be handled in supervision.

We were now placed in the position of observing the trainee co-therapists as leaders of the adolescent group. It was difficult in several ways for us to move into this new role. We felt the group "belonged" to us and that we were just lending it to the trainees to develop their skills in working with adolescents in groups. When we noticed the group progressing poorly or deteriorating because of some inappropriate input from one of our trainees, we became upset. In many respects we were seeing ourselves as novice therapists in the trainees. A new set of tensions arose around how to enable our trainees to become more competent in leading the group.

ISSUES IN SUPERVISION

Our group therapy supervision sessions began to take on the qualities of a minigroup because of this new arrangement. One of the first problems we addressed centered around the trainees' passivity in the group. Some seemed unable to establish an active leadership role, which at times kept the group from moving toward stability and cohesiveness.

Again, we shared our own experiences and presented material from the literature on group leadership. As a result, most of the trainees gained confidence and became more active in the group.

We discovered, after some frank dialogue, that some trainees felt their passivity was tied to being overwhelmed by the amount of psychopathology in the group, and to feeling inadequate to run the group according to our model and under our constant direct observation. We spent extra time in supervision working on these concerns and finally agreed that they could do several sessions without our direct observation. This approach allowed the trainees to become more active and eventually develop into quite adept group leaders.

Discussion of the activity-passivity theme helped to get other trainee struggles out on the table. The trainees began to evaluate themselves openly during supervisory sessions, and these self-assessments led to several important insights.

Some of them identified with the inpatient members in the group and did not feel competent or comfortable in confronting the adolescents when they were acting out. The type of control or parenting needed to deal with the acting out episodes was apparently very unfamiliar to them, and they saw themselves as unable to handle this area effectively.

Others were overwhelmed by the amount of emotional suffering they saw in each adolescent. In some instances, trainees could not see parallels between their own adolescent development and the problems being related by group members. Finally, a few trainees perceived the adolescents as having far more courage in dealing with certain life situations than they had in their own lives.

As the trainees disclosed more and more through their self-assessment, it became clear that the adolescent group therapy experience was making them examine their own identity issues. In this context our minigroup supervision sessions took on the flavor of supportive therapy for the trainees.

THE MIRRORING PHENOMENON

In reflecting on our minigroup supervisory sessions, we discovered a very interesting phenomenon. If our trainees were battling with issues of passive-aggressive behavior on the part of the adolescents (such as coming to group late), we would often experience similar behavior from the trainees: if the adolescent gorup had low energy and seemed to be in a rut, that mood became dominant in the minigroup; if the adolescent group contained a great deal of bitterness toward the leaders, angry confrontation would emerge from our trainees; if the group was confused or muddled, then elements of confusion would evolve later in our supervision sesison. The powerful agenda of the adolescent group therapy was being passed along verbally and behaviorally through the trainees to us as supervisors.

This mirroring phenomenon is certainly well understood in psychoanalytic treatment and in the supervision of persons training to be psychoanalysts. As supervisors using an interpersonal dynamic perspective, we began to explore how the transference material in the group among the patients and trainee co-therapist was being reenacted in the minigroup supervision. Having this transference perspective helped us immeasurably to look at ourselves as supervisors of the trainees.

In practical terms, we began labeling and summarizing the minigroup sessions in terms of process and then clarifying to what degree certain content was simply a reenactment of group transference. We then took the minigroup through these insights so that they might be mirrored back to the adolescent group.

EFFECTIVE AND INEFFECTIVE ADOLESCENT GROUP THERAPISTS

From our experience as co-therapists in the adolescent group therapy program and as supervisors of trainees, we have come to some conclusions about the specific ingredients that go into the development of effective adolescent group therapists.

Trainees who have had good supervision in working with adult groups have an edge over those whose first training experience is in adolescent groups. And those who have had personal therapy of a sophisticated nature, whether individual or group psychotherapy, for the most part have an advantage over trainees with little or none. The exception is the trainee who has had unsuccessful therapy; this individual is a high risk in doing either individual or group psychotherapy, especially with adolescent psychiatric inpatients. The trainee who is experiencing a stressful life crisis such as a divorce or a death in the family can also be at high risk as an adolescent group therapy trainee.

Essentially, we are saying that one basic ingredient for an effective adolescent group psychotherapist is that he or she have a solid personal identity and emotional maturity, whether it has come via therapy or through healthy psychological maturation.

What do we mean by solid personal identity and emotional maturity? A solid personal identity refers to a set of issues that have been mastered by the aspiring therapist during adolescence and young adulthood, including those specified by Erikson: (1) accepting one's body; (2) achieving emotional independence from parents and other adults; (3) learning a masculine or feminine role; (4) selecting and preparing for an occupation; and (5) developing both a scale of values and an ethical system (Erikson, 1963).

Emotional maturity refers to a style of interpersonal operation in which an individual is more "other person" than self-oriented, more problem solving than defensive about his or her position or view, and mostly self-directing, autonomous and interdependent, rather than overly dependent or independent in interactions with others.

Why should there be this strong emphasis on a solid personal identity and emotional maturity? In adolescent group therapy, the therapist quickly becomes a model, by his or her own behavior and reactions to group members. A well-integrated personality and emotional maturity modeled by the therapist help immeasurably in dealing with the developmental issues all adolescents face, and most particularly with those who are psychiatric inpatients.

Another characteristic we see as crucial to the effective adolescent group therapist is a genuine interest in adolescents. The population called adolescents, those between childhood and adulthood, holds particular interest for some aspiring therapists, and very little for others. It is critically important for supervisors to be able to discern the trainees' level of interest in working with adolescent psychiatric patients. If they have an obviously genuine interest and are confident that they can master the complexities of treating teenagers, that is all to the good; but if they feel ambivalent about working with this age group, it is going to be quite difficult for them to develop into competent therapists.

Of equal importance is a firm belief that group psychotherapy is the best way to treat adolescents. Trainees can come to this resolve from their own experiences in group, reading about therapy, observing ongoing adolescent groups, or a combination of these. Without a strong conviction that the group psychotherapy approach is an eminently sensible and powerful method of helping troubled adolescents, the trainee is much less likely to become an effective adolescent group therapist.

Finally, in terms of inherent attributes, it is central that the trainee manifest personal growth and honesty, together with a sense of psychological well-being. Personal warmth has been noted by Strupp (1962), Collier and Defer (1975), and Mendelsohn, Yates, and Peterson (1957) as leading to favorable diagnostic and prognostic expectations and a greater communication of empathy.

Being a warm therapist with adolescents increases rapport and mutual trust between group members and the therapist. Many adolescent psychiatric inpatients have not seen empathetic interpersonal transactions or experienced empathy themselves. Having a therapist with a strong capacity for empathy will enable the adolescents to develop this component in their own lives.

Honesty when dealing with adolescents is also vitally important. We mentioned earlier that a part of the identity process for the adolescent is the establishment of an ethical system. In supervising trainees, we have consistently observed that adolescents in group will test the value system of the therapist over and over again. They will ask the therapist's opinions about many matters with ethical or moral overtones, such as taking drugs, violating trust in relationships, sexual behavior, stealing, or cheating in school.

When these matters are brought up in group by the adolescent, they represent areas of concern and insecurity. How the therapist handles these matters gives the adolescents an index of his degree of honesty or corruption. If the therapist has the courage to reveal how he has dealt with these issues or has enabled other adolescents to deal with them, the potential for developing high credibility has been set in place. If, on the other hand, the therapist reveals personal dishonesty or colludes with a position, attitude, or behavior that is harmful to the adolescent, this dishonesty will be brought up again and again in therapy.

In many respects, the adolescent wants to be able to discover from the therapist an approach to developing an ethical framework without merely taking over the system of the therapist verbatim. If the therapist gives a flippant or sarcastic response to questions of this nature, the adolescent will know that the therapist is probably in the same predicament she is regarding that particular matter. If the therapist is vague, anxious, or confused when responding, the adolescent will think the therapist is incompetent or unwilling to share his approach.

What knowledge base about adolescent psychology, psychotherapy, and psychopathology should an effective therapist have? We have often observed a warm, caring, and honest trainee giving information or opinions from an experiential or an opinion base that may be less accurate or relevant than those of peers, parents, or teachers of the adolescent. During these interactions it was apparent that the trainee's status as a therapist decreased dramatically. We thus make a very strong case that detailed, factual material about adolescent development is needed before the trainee goes into group therapy with adolescents.

Specifically, let us consider what we think minimal for a trainee therapist to be equipped with before having a group experience. Foremost is a good understanding of normal adolescent development, which could be obtained by takng courses in developmental psychology or psychology of adolescents, or simply by reading material on adolescent development. Having a working knowledge of the normal adolescent developmental process is as important as understanding adolescent psychopathology.

An awareness of themes in adolescence is equally essential; one can recall some of these themes from one's own life as a useful exercise. We have often been amazed by trainees who seem unable to recollect important aspects of their own adolescence. Time and again we have seen adolescents in therapy who have been either undertreated or over-treated by clinicians who really had little depth of information about normal or abnormal adolescent functioning.

Adolescents themselves make systematic judgments of the therapist's competence based on their behavior and particularly on the type of questions the therapist asks. Questions as well as answers reveal a great deal about the adolescent group therapist.

The trainee needs a therapy framework from which to operate when treating adolescents in group therapy. The notion of getting a group of troubled adolescents together and just sitting in a room, waiting to see what happens, is not only naive and unsophisticated therapeutically but dangerous to the mental health of all involved. Thus trainees need to realize that therapy is a process that moves through predictable stages; they need to know something of group dynamics, possibly from an experiential basis, but also from course work and reading; and they could certainly benefit from discussing books on adolescent group therapy with experienced therapists.

Finally, effective therapists of adolescents usually have had in their own adolescence a rich and meaningful set of experiences from which to draw. They see themes of adolescence (e.g., the dominance-submission conflict, independence-dependence interaction, value conflicts, and sexual struggles) not only in highly intellectualized, clinical terms but from a humanistic standpoint as well. If the trainee's own healthy adolescent period of development is not clearly available while leading a therapy group, very little empathy or understanding will be communicated to the patients.

What about the characteristics of ineffective adolescent group therapists? We could simply say that levels of ineffectiveness increase if the trainee does not have the personal attributes, skills, and knowledge just outlined for the effective therapist. And to some degree this proposition is true; however, the problem is not quite so simple.

We have seen characteristics and behaviors that are extremely detrimental to adolescent group work. If the trainee is very insecure as a person or professional and has to hide behind her educational degrees or training, adopting a rather arbitrary and authoritarian position in dealing with adolescents in groups, then a poor therapy outcome will ensue.

Adolescents, including psychiatric inpatients, are not adults and do not have a great deal of respect for mental health professionals' degrees. Many disturbed adolescents in group psychotherapy have acted out in serious ways against their parents and teachers and usually see little reason not to carry on this same behavior with mental health professionals, particularly if they are confronted in a power struggle because of titles or degrees.

Being too loving and accepting—in a sense being a masochistic therapist—leads to ineffective therapy. As ridiculous as the position may appear, some trainees believe that if they allow disturbed adolescents to do whatever they wish, somehow their mental health will improve. If an adult trainee cannot defend herself creatively and successfully in adolescent group therapy, it does great harm to the therapy process, creating chaos, psychological suffering, and more aberrant behavior on the part of the teenagers in the group.

Taking a somewhat sadistic approach can also be highly detrimental. Some trainees adopt a quasi-analytic theoretical stance out of their own insecurity and victimize their patients through the use of professional jargon and detachment. This process consists of a power game by the trainee in an attempt to distance himself or herself from the disturbed patients. Adolescents react very unfavorably to this victimization and, in most instances, come to distrust the trainee's interest or concern for them.

Another unproductive style is that of befriending or buddying up to the patients. Most healthy as well as disturbed adolescents greet this condescending posture as perplexing and not useful in helping them move toward adulthood. Some ineffective trainees, for example, became advocates of the adolescent inpatients' "rights," so that ultimately all semblance to group therapy was absent. These group leaders continued the "rights" issue even in our group supervisory sessions.

We often found ourselves using techniques in the minigroup that we were trying to teach the trainees to use in their group sessions with the adolescents. The co-therapist dialogue and the dilemma approach were two successful approaches.

The ineffectual therapists were characterized generally as having some personality component—rigidity, a dogmatic view of adolescents, dishonesty, excessive fearfulness, or lack of warmth, care, or concern—that emerged as a clear impediment to working with adolescents in group. The components also led to control issues in supervision, a lack of openness to feedback, and, consequently, a lack of growth both personally and as therapists.

Fortunately, the vast majority of our trainees developed skills in the adequate-to-excellent range, and only about 10 percent fell into the category of ineffective. At the end of our supervisory relationship, we gave trainees precise feedback about their work with the adolescents, centered on their unique competencies, gifts, and talents, and those deficits and blind spots that still needed work.

SUMMARY

Averill's work at the Boys' Industrial School provided a useful set of therapeutic goals for adolescent group therapy with male delinquents, a set of instructions for group psychotherapists, and a list of insights the psychotherapists hoped to pass on to the patients. All these materials were similar to what evolved in our adolescent group therapy programs at the Hall Institute.

Specifying our expectations and goals for the patients, the therapeutic process, and the learning experiences for the trainees improved the overall functioning of the adolescent group therapy program. This contributed to our understanding of effective and ineffective adolescent group therapists and helped us as supervisors to concentrate on problems that evolved in our supervisory minigroup.

11

SUMMARY AND IMPLICATIONS

Endure, and preserve yourself for brighter things.

—Virgil
Aeneid

In summarizing and drawing conclusions from our model of adolescent group therapy, we need to address several important issues. First, we need to reflect on the factors that influenced the development of our model so as to examine what we have learned in the process of developing this model. Second, it is essential that we sum up what we see as the significant components of the model. Next, we want to consider some implications for our model as it is used in different contexts with populations of teenagers who are not in psychiatric treatment. Finally, we will offer some research questions that might prove useful to those practitioners who also do group research.

As we sum up and consider the implications, we should remember that our model of adolescent group therapy as presented is not static and is not completely developed, but is ready to be shared with other practitioners and researchers.

INFLUENCING FACTORS

In developing our model, we learned that adolescent group therapy has an important history, that it is anchored in Moreno's (1932) psychodrama, Adler's (1930) clinics, and Aichhorn's (1935) group work with aggresive youngsters. As we did our work as group therapists, it became clear that Slavson's (1943) mandate—that successful adolescent group therapists must be more active than adult group therapists—was highly accurate. It also became clear that our roles and activities as adolescent group therapists needed to be guided by theoretical rationales that are quite diverse: sometimes psychodynamic, sometimes behavioral or developmental-interpersonal, sometimes existential.

We need to keep in mind that our model is really the product of the 1970s and 1980s, as mentioned in earlier chapters. The professional zeitgeist for working with teenagers in group therapy was very supportive, particularly during the 1970s, and the Child and Adolescent Service of the William S. Hall Psychiatric Institute was very supportive in our efforts to develop a group therapy program. As maturing co-therapists and supervisors of trainees, we incorporated our interest in family therapy, normal adolescent development, and the promotion of social competency into our model of group therapy. When we started to use the group process to encourage social competency development in each group member, our definition of social competency came into focus: A unique set of self-perceptions and interpersonal skills that fosters the development of meaningful relationships and the mastery of significant life events and that moves the adolescent toward a level of maturity and healthy "self-parenting" sufficient to meet the challenges of adulthood. Our definition takes into consideration each teenager's uniqueness as well as the dynamic developmental process involved in the establishment of an identity and in moving toward healthy autonomy in adulthood.

Looking at our adolescent group over time, we discovered it had identifiable stages and phases, which we have described in table 1. These stages involved movement from environmental issues to personal issues and at times to a purely group focus. Our model was very useful in helping co-therapists get a sense of where they were in the development of their groups and how to intervene prescriptively to advance the group functioning.

As we reflect on our co-therapy relationship, we see that choosing one another as co-therapists was a powerful factor that influenced the model that emerged. We persisted in giving one another feedback, developing strategies and tactics to deal with changes and resistances in the group process.

An additional factor influencing the development of our model was the realization that much of the resistance encountered in group sessions was essentially a method by which the adolescents were communicating their respective histories to the group. We began to see the resistances as important building blocks for the group's development.

In supervising adolescent group therapy trainees, we discovered the essence of our therapy model. The clinical psychology interns, child psychiatry fellows, and general psychiatry residents whom we supervised requested that we write down aspects of our model to serve as a guide in their group work. The resulting manual was a precursor to this book. As the manual was transformed into the book, we broadened our awareness of the role that the literature on adolescent group therapy, both the empirical and theoretical, played in developing our model.

SIGNIFICANT COMPONENTS

The significant components of our adolescent group therapy model include: (1) characteristics and expected behaviors of the adolescents in the group, (2) characteristics and expected behaviors of the co-therapist, (3) strategies and tactics to prevent group regression, and (4) strategies and tactics to maintain high levels of group functioning through the promotion of social competency.

Once the group screening process was in place, the adolescents admitted to our group were male and female psychiatric inpatients between the ages of 15 and 19. Their intellectual functioning ranged from low average to superior, and a large percentage of the adolescents were free of severe psychopathology. In the group sessions they were expected to verbalize, mention something about themselves, listen to other group members, and enter into group discussions.

The co-therapists in the group were adult male and female mental health professionals strongly motivated to work with adolescent psychiatric inpatients in a group context. The co-therapists treated one another as co-equal professionals in terms of the leadership roles, and they operated (or were expected to operate) in a complementary and highly synchronized manner, being active, warm, and expressive in order to promote an optimal group atmosphere. Each therapist was expected to exhibit a wide range of behaviors while interacting with the group. Some of the expert therapist behaviors could be labelled tough, tender, sensitive, confrontational, reflective, understanding, and curious.

As the group progressed over time, specific strategies and tactics were developed to prevent episodes of recurrent regression. These strategies and tactics included methods for disarming negative group leaders, interventions to redistribute power among group members, and a refined screening of group candidates. The strategy of ritualizing the process by which adolescents and therapists entered or departed the group was a major component in preventing group regression. The strategies of the modified fishbowl also helped stabilize and move the group through a very precarious time.

The tactics and strategies that were essential components to maintaining optimal group functioning include co-therapist dialogue, co-therapist dilemma processing, and co-therapist transition to a more reflective consultant role. As co-therapists began to talk directly to each other in the group there was a dramatic shift to more stability in the group process. This dialogue apepared to allow some adolescent members, perhaps for the first time, to see how adults could cooperate and collaborate in solving problems in a group situation.

With the co-therapist dialogue in place, the co-therapists began to use a dilemma-processing strategy to deal more effecively with the resistances that emerged. Enabling group members to talk out their dilemmas, rather than act them out, provided a strong impetus for the promotion of social competency. As the group members took more control of themselves, the process and content of the group were at an optimal level. The co-therapists at this point became less active and directing, and became more removed—playing a consultant role. The group as a whole functioned in a very sensitive, caring, and competent level with the courage to process very complex issues in a highly competent manner.

NEW SETTINGS

We have indicated that our model was developed within an adolescent inpatient context. Currently, it continues to be used with adolescent psychiatric inpatients at the William S. Hall Psychiatric Institute and has expanded its use to adolescent psychiatric outpatients at the institute. The success we have had in these settings strongly supports using the model in additional settings, specifically in public and private high schools, in juvenile delinquency facilities, and with youth groups in churches or synagogues.

In terms of public or private high schools, the model might be incorporated as part of the curriculum. Using male and female group leader teams trained in techniques outlined in this book, these new experiential groups would be part of the curriculum during all four years of high school. In the first year the group would consist of an introduction to adolescent life development, in the sophomore and junior years intermediate adolescent life development, and in the senior year advanced adolescent life development.

This type of curriculum would offer teenagers a formal and regular context to process many of their struggles with growing up. In this application of the model, the students would have sensitive, caring adults in their lives and peer interaction on a consistent basis. This would offer socially neglected and socially rejected teenagers a psychologically healthy forum that would replace the dysfunctional interactions experienced at home and in other areas of school. Further, it would relieve the burden of teachers who, despite limited time and resources, try to care sensitively for youngsters who see teachers as the only significant functioning adult in their lives. Bringing the model to the school curriculum has the potential to prevent some of the psychiatric and anti-social problems we have worked with in our inpatient and outpatient psychiatric populations.

In juvenile delinquency facilities there are special problems within that population concerning issues of security, impulsive acting-out, difficulties in solving problems with words rather than actions, and a history of few success experiences in coping with society. Additionally, much of the public and many institutions believe that the juvenile delinquency population is an untreatable group of adolescents. We suggest that our model might be adapted for some of these juvenile delinquents who are not extremely impulsive and who are open to learning new ways to solve problems and deal with conflicts.

For church and synagogue youth groups we see the model as being readily adaptable. Youngsters in these groups need the opportunity to discuss, in depth, issues they are trying to manage. In some existing youth groups there are attempts to provide lectures, guided discussions, and field trips to promote healthy psychological functioning. All of these activities have value for the developing teenager's psychological and spiritual growth. The model would complement and enhance these activities by having a strong emphasis on listening to individual and group concerns that the group members might generate. Listening and dialoguing with functional young people permit growth and development that move them toward self-realization and self-actualization rather than simply overcoming social deficits.

IMPLICATIONS FOR RESEARCH

Our model of adolescent group therapy was developed and refined from a clinical intervention perspective and as a clinical model to teach trainees how to do adolescent group therapy. We have clinical data, in the form of patient self-reports, staff observations, and parent and teacher reports, that certian skills and competencies developed in group were being used by our patients in other settings, such as in school, with their families, and in peer relationships. At this time we are researching ways to alter the model in working with outpatient adolescents as opposed to inpatient adolescents. We are gaining feedback about the effectiveness of the model with youngsters who have a much shorter inpatient stay than those hospitalized for extended periods. Our research program involves both content and process studies; outcome studies involving self-reports, family reports, and behavioral observations of change as noted by staff, family, school, and peers; studies examining the interaction between personality variables and group behavior; and studies of the impact of specific interventions on group satisfaction and group problem solving.

As the model is used in other settings, we strongly urge that research components always be included. For example, if the model were used in a high school over a four-year period, it would be important to ask several research questions: In what ways does the model need to be adjusted to fit successfully into the traditional curriculum of a high school? Once implemented, how does the high school using the model compare with a similar high school that does not have an experiential group component? The high schools could be compared on issues such as attendance, frequency of fighting, pregnancy rates, disruptive classroom behavior, and property destruction. If the model implemented in the school is working successfully in terms of promoting social competency we would predict a decrease in many of those behaviors.

In juvenile delinquency facilities, the model could be used immediately with those teenagers who have the most impulse control. From a research perspective, a thorough screening system would identify significant personal characteristics of prospective group members. For those teenagers with a moderate level of impulsivity, having an extended time of observing adolescent group therapy would perhaps enable them to become suitable candidates for actual participation in a group. This observing process would be similar to the modified fishbowl intervention that we used as one point in the development of our approach.

In using the model with church or synagogue youth groups, several research questions are raised. In working with healthy well-functioning adolescents, what similarities and differences do we observe when they are compared with dysfunctional teenagers in formal treatment? Does the model have the potential to move adolescents who are already functioning well to a high level of ego integration? Does the model help teenagers who are members of a youth group and who are going through developmental crises or family crises to manage more effectively than those lacking a group experience.

In closing, we set out to write a book describing our model of adolescent group therapy. There have been periods of genuine joy and periods of anguish in maturing as group therapists and in writing this book, but in retrospect, we feel positive about what we have written and about what we have learned from our group members, adolescents, and trainees over the years. It is our hope that what we have shared will prove useful to other clinicians and researchers working with teenagers.

REFERENCES

Achenbach, T. M., and Edelbrock, C. S. (1971). Behavioral problems and competencies reported by parents of normal and disturbed children aged four through sixteen. *Social Research and Child Development, 46* 1-82.

Adler, A. (1930). *Guiding the child.* New York: Greenberg Publishing.

Aichhorn, A. (1935). *Wayward youth.* New York: Viking Press.

Aichhorn, A. (1964). *Delinquency and child guidance: Selected papers.* New York: International Universities Press.

Ainsworth, M. D., Blehar, M. C., Waters, E., & Wall, S. (1978). *Patterns of attachment: A psychological study of the strange situation.* Hillsdale, NJ: Lawrence Erlbaum.

Anthony, E. J. (1968). Reflections on twenty-five years of group psychotherapy. *Internatinal Journal of Group Psychotherapy, 18,* 277-301.

Argyle, M., & Dean, J. (1965). Eye-contact, distance and affiliation. *Sociometry, 28,* 289-304.

Averill, S. C., Cadman, W. H., Craig, L., & Linden, R. E. (1973). Group psychotherapy with young delinquents: Report from a residential treatment center. *Bulletin of the Menninger Clinic, 37,* 15-34.

Bales, R. F. (1950). *Interaction process analysis: A method for the study of small groups.* Reading, MA: Addison Wesley.

Bandura, A. (1960). *Relationship of family patterns to child behavior disorders: A progress report.* Stanford, CA: Stanford University Press.

Bandura, A. (1969). *Principles of behavior modification.* New York: Holt, Rinehart & Winston.

Bardill, D. R. (1977). A behavior-contracting program of group treatment for early adolescents in a residential treatment setting. *International Journal of Group Psychotherapy, 27,* 389-400.

Bartlett, J. (1980). *Familiar quotations.* Boston: Little, Brown.

Baumrind, D. (1966). Effects of authoritative parental control on child behavior. *Child Development, 37,* 887-907.

Baumrind, D. (1968). Authoritarian versus authoritative parental control. *Adolescence, 3,* 255-272.

Baumrind, D. (1978). Parental disciplinary patterns and social competence in children. *Youth and Society, 9,* 239-276.

Beitel, A., Everts, P., Boile, B., Nagel, E., Bragdon, C., & Mackesson, B. (1983). Hub group: An innovative approach to group therapy in a short-term inpatient adolescent unit. *Adolescence, 18,* 1-15.

Bender, L., & Schilder, P. (1937). Suicidal preoccupation and attempts in children. *American Journal of Orthopsychiatry, 7,* 225-234.

Berkovitz, I. (Ed.). (1972). *Adolescents grow in groups: Experiences in adolescent group psychotherapy.* New York: Brunner/Mazel.

Berkovitz, I., & Sugar, M. (1976). An experience in teaching adolescent group psychotherapy: Observers become participants. *International Journal of Group Psychotherapy, 26,* 441-453.

Bernard, H., Babineau, R., & Schwartz, A. (1980). Supervisor-trainee cotherapy as a method for individual psychotherapy training. *Psychiatry, 43,* 138-145.

Bernard, H. S., Drob, S. & Lifshutz, H. (1987). Complaining between cotherapists: An empirical report. *Psychotherapy, 24*(1), 96-104.

Bernet, W. (1982). The technique of verbal games in group therapy with early adolescents. *Journal of the American Academy of Child Psychiatry, 21,* 496-501.

Bion, W. R. (1961). *Experiences in groups, and other papers.* New York: Basic Books.

Bloom, V., & Dobie, S. (1969). The effects of observers on the process of group therapy. *International Journal of Group Psychotherapy, 19,* 79-87.

Bowers, W. A., & Gauron, E. F. (1981). Potential hazards of the co-therapy relationship. *Psychotherapy: Theory, Research and Practice, 18,* 225-228.

Bowlby, J. (1977). The making and breaking of affectional bonds. *British Journal of Psychiatry, 130,* 201-210.

Bowlby, J. (1988). Developmental psychiatry comes of age. *American Journal of Psychiatry, 145,* 1-10.

Bowlby, J., & Parkes, C. M. (1970). Separation and loss within the family. In E. J. Anthony & C. Koupernik (Eds.), *The child and his family* (Vol. 1). New York: John Wiley.

Bretherton, I. (1985). Attachment theory: Retrospect and prospect. In I. Bretherton & E. Waters (Eds.), Growing points in attachment theory and research. *Monograph of the Society for Research in Child Development, 50* (Serial No. 209).

Brockbank, R. (1980). Adolescent psychodynamics and the therapy group. *Adolescent Psychiatry, 8,* 529-538.

Buscaglia, L. (1985). *Love.* New York: Fawcett Crest.

Collier, G., and Defer, B. (1975). Various biological changes seen during reserpine therapy. *Annales Medico-Psychologiques, 1,* 901-911.

Corder, B. F. (1975). A structured activity to facilitate group psychotherapy. *North Carolina Journal of Mental Health, 2,* 42-45.

Corder, B. F., Russell, R., & Koehne, P. (Winter, 1984-85). A format for evaluating group process and co-therapy functioning in adolescent therapy groups. *Psychiatric Forum,* 22-27.

Corder, B. F., Whiteside, L., & Haizlip, T. M. (1981). A study of curative factors in group psychotherapy with adolescents. *International Journal of Group Psychotherapy, 31,* 345-354.

Corder, B. F., Whiteside, R., & Vogel, M. (1977). A therapeutic game for structuring and facilitating group psychotherapy with adolescents. *Adolescence, 46,* 261-267.

Corsini, R. J., & Rosenberg, B. (1955). Mechanisms of group psychotherapy. *Journal of Abnormal and Social Psychology,51,* 406-411.

Davis, F. B., & Lohr, N. E. (1971). Special problems with the use of cotherapists in group psychotherapy. *International Journal of Group Psychotherapy, 21,* 143-158.

Erikson, E. (1963). *Childhood and society.* New York: Norton.

Erikson, E. (1968). *Identity, youth and crisis.* New York: Norton.

Fiendler, E. L., Ecton, R. B., Kingsley, D., & Dubey, D. R. (1986). Group anger control training for institutionalized psychiatric male adolescents. *Behavior Therapy, 17,* 109-123.

Fine, S., Knight-Webb, G., & Breau, K. (1976). Volunteer adolescents in adolescent group therapy: Effects on patients and volunteers. *British Journal of Psychiatry, 129,* 407-413.

Fine, S., Knight-Webb, G., & Vernon, J. (1977). Selected volunteer adolescents in adolescent group therapy. *Adolescence, 46,* 189-197.

Frances, A., & Schiff, M. (1976). Popular music as a catalyst in the induction of therapy groups for teenagers. *International Journal of Group Psychotherapy, 26,* 391-398.

Freud, S. (1948). *Group psychology and the analysis of the ego.* London: Hogarth Press.

Gantman, C. A. (1978). Family interaction patterns among families with normal, disturbed, and drug-abusing adolescents. *Journal of Youth and Adolescence, 7,* 429-440.

Gardner, R. A. (1975). *Psychotherapeutic approaches to the resistant child.* New York: Jason Aronson.

Garmezy, N., & Masten, A. (1986). Stress, competence, and resilience: Common frontiers for therapist and psychopathology. *Behavior Therapy, 17,* 500-521.

Ginnott, H. (1958). Play group psychotherapy: A theoretical framework. *International Journal of Group Psychotherapy, 86,* 410-418.

Golden, D. L. & Dominak, G. M. (1986). Single-gender group psychotherapy: A "womans group" for adolescent inpatients. *Group, 10,* 217-227.

Goodman, G. (1967). An experiment with companionship therapy: College students and troubled boys—assumptions, selections and design. *American Journal of Public Health, 57,* 1772-1777.

Greenblum, D. N., & Pinney, E. L. (1982). Some comments on the role of cotherapists in group psychotherapy with borderline patients. *Group, 6,* 41-47.

Hall, E. T. (1966). *The hidden dimension.* Garden City, NY:. Doubleday.

Hamburg, B., & Verenhorst, B. (1972). Peer counseling in the secondary schools: A community health project for youth. *American Journal of Orthopsychiatry, 42,* 566-581.

Harlow, H. (1958). The nature of love. *American Psychologist, 13,* 673-685.

Hartup, W. W. (1989). Social relationships and their developmental significance. *American Psychologist, 44,* 120-126.

Hartup, W. W., Laursen, B., Stewart, M. I., & Eastenson, A. (1988). A conflict and the friendship relations of young children. *Child Development, 59,* 1590-1600.

Heckel, R. V., Holmes, G. R., & Rosecrans, C. J. (1971). A factor analytic study of group process variables. *Journal of Clinical Psychology, 27,* 146-150.

Heckel, R. V., & Salzberg, H. C. (1967). Predicting verbal behavioral change in group therapy using a screening scale. *Psychological Reports, 20,* 403-406.

Hellwig, K., & Memmot, R. J. (1974). Cotherapy: The balancing act. *Small Group Behavior, 5,* 175-181.

Hurst, A. G., Stein, K. B., Korchin, S. J., & Soskin, W. F. (1978). Leadership style determinants of cohesiveness in adolescent groups. *International Journal of Group Psychotherapy, 28, 28,* 263-277.

Jourard, S. M. (1968). *Disclosing man to himself.* New York: Van Nostrand Reinhold.

Kaplan, D., & Phillips, M. (1981). *Cheers* (Inspirational Series). Atlanta: M & L Sales, 1-96.

Kerfoot, M. (1980). The family context of adolescent suicidal behavior. *Journal of Adolescence, 3,* 335-346.

Klein, R. H., Brown, S. L., & Hunter, D.E.K. (1986). Long-term inpatient group psychotherapy: The ward group. *International Journal of Group Psychtherapy, 36,* 361-380.

Kobasa, S. C. (1979). Stressful life events, personality and health: An inquiry into hardiness. *Journal of Personality and Social Psychology, 37,* 1-11.

Lundin, W. H., & Aranov, B. M. (1952). The use of co-therapists in group psychotherapy. *Journal of Consulting Psychology, 16,* 76-80.

MacLennan, B., & Felsenfeld, N. (1968). *Group counseling and psychotherapy with adolescents.* New York: Columbia University Press.

Marsh, L. C. (1935). Group therapy and the psychiatric clinic. *Journal of Nervous and Mental Diseases, 82,* 381-392.

Martin, E. A., & Hill, W. F. (1957). Toward a theory of group development. *Internatinal Journal of Group Psychotherapy, 7,* 20-30.

Maslow, A. H., & Mintz, N. L. (1956). Effects of esthetic surroundings: Initial effects of three esthetic conditions upon perceiving "energy" and "well-being" in faces. *Journal of Psychology, 41,* 247-254.

Mavrit, R. C., Lind, J., & McLaughlin, D. G. (1974). Use of videotape to induce change in delinquent adolescents. *American Journal of Psychiatry, 131,* 996-999.

Maxmen, J. S. (1973). Group therapy as viewed by hospitalized patients. *Archives of General Psychiatry, 28,* 404-408.

Mazza, N. (1981). The use of poetry in treating the troubled adolescent. *Adolescence, 16,* 403-408.

McMahon, N., & Links, P. S. (1984). Cotherapy: The need for positive pairing. *Canadian Journal of Psychiatry, 29,* 385-389.

Mehrabian, A. (1971). Nonverbal communication. In M. R. Jones (Ed.). Nebraska symposium on motivation. Lincoln: University of Nebraska Press.

Mendelsohn, R. M., Yates, J. W., & Peterson, L. (1957). The experiential aspect of psychotherapy. *American Journal of Psychotherapy, 11,* 254-261.

Miller, D. H. (1973). The drug-dependent adolescent. *Adolescent Psychotherapy, 2,* 70-97.

Mintz, E. (1963). Special values of co-therapists in group psychotherapy. *International Journal of Group Psychotherapy, 13,* 127-132.

Mintz, E. (1965). Male-female co-therapists: Some values and some problems. *American Journal of Psychotherapy, 19,* 293-301.

Mintz, N. L. (1956). Effects of esthetic surroundings: Prolonged repeated experience in a "beautiful" and "ugly" room. *Journal of Psychology, 41,* 459-466.

Moreno, J. L. (1932). Application of the group method to classification. *National Commission on Prisons and Prison Labor.*

Mullan, H., & Rosenbaum, M. (1953). *Group psychotherapy,* New York: Ronald.

Napier, R., & Gersehnfeld, M. (1973). *Groups: Theory and experience.* Boston: Houghton Mifflin.

Nicholi, A. M. (1985). Commitment to family. *Family building,* Ventura, CA: Regal Books.

Oldham, J. M. (1982). The use of silent observers as an adjunct to short-term inpatient group psychotherapy. *International Journal of Group Psychotherapy, 32,* 469-480.

Olsson, P. A., & Myers, I. L. (1972). Nonverbal techniques in an adolescent group. *International Journal of Group Psychotherapy, 22,* 186-191.

Paterson, R. J., & Moran, G. (1988). Attachment theory, personality development, and psychotherapy. *Clinical Psychology Review, 8,* 611-636.

Patterson, M. (1987). Presentational and affect management functions of nonverbal involvement. *Journal of Nonverbal Behavior, 11,* 110-122.

Paulson, I., Burroughs, J. C., & Gelb, C. G. (1976). Cotherapy: What is the crux of the relationship? *International Journal of Group Psychotherapy, 26,* 213-224.

Piaget, J., & Inhelder, B. *The psychology of the child.* New York: Basic Books.

Rachman, A., & Heller, M. (1976). Peer group psychotherapy with adolescent drug abusers. *International Journal of Group Psychotherapy, 26,* 373-384.

Rachman, A., & Raubolt, R. (1984). The pioneers of adolescent group psychotherapy. *International Journal of Group Psychotherapy, 34,* 387-413.

Rawson, H., & Miner, M. (1986). *The new international dictionary of quotations.* New York: E. P. Dutton.

Rohrbough, M., & Bartels, B. D. (1975). Participants' perceptions of curative factors in therapy and growth groups. *Small Group Behavior, 6,* 430-456.

Rosenbaum, M., & Berger, M. (1963). *Group psychotherapy and group function: Selected readings.* New York: Basic Books.

Rosenstock,. H. A., & McLaughlin, M. (1982). Positive group efficacy in adolescent treatment. *Journal of Clinical Psychiatry, 43,* 58-60.

Rosenthal, L. (1971). Some dynamics and therapeutic management in adolescent group therapy. *Psychoanalytic Review, Fall,* 353-366.

Rutan, J. S., & Alonso, A. (1980). Sequential cotherapy of groups for training and clinical care. *Group, 4,* 40-50.

Rutter, M. (1979). Maternal deprivation 1972-1978 new findings, new concepts, new approaches. *Child Development, 50,* 283-305.

Rutter, M. (1981). Stress, coping and development: Some issues and some questions. *Journal of Child Psychology and Psychiatry, 22,* 323-356.

Rutter, M. (1985). Resilience in the face of adversity. Protective factors and resistance to psychiatric disorder. *British Journal of Psychiatry, 147,* 511-598.

Rutter, M., Quinton, D., & Liddle, C. (1983). Parenting in two generations: Looking backwards and looking forwards. In N. Madge (Ed.), *Families at risk.* London: Heinemann.

Saffer, J. B. (1986). Group therapy with friends of an adolescent suicide. *Adolescence, 21,* 743-745.

Schilder, P. (1939). Results and problems of group psychotherapy in severe neurosis. *Mental Hygiene, 23,* 87-98.

Schwartzberg, A., Mullens, B. N. & Grace, M. M. (1971, July). Diagnostic groups in an adolescent treatment program. *Hospital and Community Psychiatry,* 217-219.

Shainess, N. (1977). Conscience and the psychotherapeutic pursuit. *Voices, 13,* 36-39.

Slavson, S. R. (1943). *An introduction to group therapy.* New York: Commonwealth Fund.

Slavson, S. R. (1958). *Child-centered group guidance of parents.* New York: International Universities Press.

Smets, A. C., & Cebula, C. M. (1987). A group treatment program for adolescent sex offenders: Five steps toward resolution. *Child Abuse & Neglect, 11,* 247-254.

Solnit, A. J., Settlage, C. F., Gookman, S., & Blas, P. (1969). Youth unrest: A symposium. *American Journal of Psychiatry, 125,* 1145-1159.

Spitz, R. (1945). Hospitalism: An inquiry into the genesis of psychiatric conditions in early childhood. *Psychoanalytic Study of the Child, 1,* 53-74.

Sroufe, L. A. (1979). The coherence of individual development. *American Psychologist, 34,* 834-841.

Sroufe, L. A. (1985). Attachment classification from the perspective of infant-caregiver relationships and infant temperament. *Child Development, 56,* 1-14.

Sroufe, L. A., Jacobvitz, D., Mangelsdorf, S., DeAngelo, E., & Ward, M. J. (1985). Generational boundary dissolution between mothers and their preschool children: A relationship systems approach. *Child Development, 56,* 317-325.

Stevenson, B. (1967). *The home book of quotations.* New York: Dodd, Mead.

Strupp, H. H. (1962). The therapist's contribution to the treatment process: Beginnings and vagaries of a research program. In H. H. Strupp and L. Luborsky, *Research in psychotherapy.* Washington, D.C.: American Psychological Association, Inc.

Stumphauzer, J. (1976). Modifying delinquent behavior: Beginning and current practices. *Adolescence, 41,* 13-28.

Sugar, M. (Ed.). (1975). *The adolescent in group and family therapy.* New York: Brunner/Mazel.

Sullivan, H. S. (1953). *The interpersonal theory of psychiatry.* New York: W. W. Norton.

Toker, E. (1972). The scapegoat as an essential group phenomenon. *International Journal of Group Psychotherapy, 22,* 320-332.

Tuckman, B. W. (1965). Development sequence in small groups. *Psychological Bulletin, 63,* 384-399.

Weber, L. (1980). The effect of videotape and playback on an in-patient adolescent group. *International Journal of Group Psychotherapy, 30,* 213-227.

Wender, L. (1936). The dynamics of group psychotherapy and its application. *Journal of Nervous and Mental Diseases, 84,* 54-60.

Whitaker, C. A., & Lieberman, M. (1964). *Psychotherapy through the group process.* Englewood Cliffs, NJ: Prentice-Hall.

White, R. W. (1976). *The enterprise of living: A view of personal growth* (2nd ed.). New York: Holt, Rinehart & Winston.

Winnicott, D. W. (1972) Adolescence: Struggling through the doldrums. *Adolescent Psychiatry, 1,* 40-50.

Wolf, M. (1975). Room size, group size and density: Behavior patterns in a children's psychiatric facility. *Environment and Behavior, 1,* 199-224.

Yalom, I. D. (1970). *The theory and practice of group psychotherapy.* New York: Basic Books.

AUTHOR INDEX

SUBJECT INDEX

About the Authors

GEORGE R. HOLMES is Professor of Neuropsychiatry and Behavioral Science at the University of South Carolina School of Medicine and Chief of Child and Adolescent Psychology at the William S. Hall Psychiatric Institute. He has published numerous articles in a wide range of journals, including the *Journal of Consulting and Clinical Psychology* and the *American Journal of Psychiatry*.

ROBERT V. HECKEL is Professor of Psychology at the University of South Carolina. He is author of 22 books and monographs on clinical psychology.

LUCILLE GORDON has a private practice and is Executive Director of the United Behavioral Clinics of Columbia.